DATE DUE

COSTA RICA

THE LAST COUNTRY THE GODS MADE

PHOTOGRAPHY by KIMBERLY PARSONS

TEXT by ADRIAN COLESBERRY and BRASS McLEAN

SkyHouse Publishers

Library of Congress Catalog Card Number: 93-71977

ISBN: 1-56044-191-7

Published by SkyHouse Publishers, an imprint of
Falcon Press Publishing Co., Inc., Helena, Montana,
in cooperation with Viewfinder, 435 Brannan Street,
Suite 203, San Francisco, California 94107.

Design, typesetting and other prepress work
by Falcon Graphics, Helena, Montana.

Distributed by Falcon Press Publishing Co., Inc.,
P.O. Box 1718, Helena, Montana 59624,
phone 1-800-582-2665.

Manufactured in Singapore

First Edition

For my mom, my dad, and my sister—*photographer*

———— & ————

To the green sea turtle who twenty-five years ago

bumped the bottom of a boat in Key West, Florida,

scaring a little girl. Those tears and this book

are for you and your descendants—*authors*

Table of Contents

Acknowledgments

*T*hanks a million to those who aided me,

directly or indirectly, knowingly or unknowingly, with this

project. Without them, this would never have made it to print.

Thanks to Deborah, for her unfaltering faith and wisdom;

to Ray and the gang at Pro Camera, San Francisco, California;

to the New Lab, San Francisco, California;

to Kim and Kim at Century Travel, Austin, Texas;

to Barbara, Elizabeth, Joey, Laura, Lily, M.J., Scottie, and Sheri.

— the photographer

vi

The natural history of Costa Rica began 65,000,000 years ago, about twenty miles off the country's Pacific coast, at an underwater formation called the Middle America Trench. The trench marks the boundary between the Cocos Plate, a section of the ocean floor moving northeast, and the Caribbean Plate, a sedentary section of continental crust that includes Costa Rica. Each year, the Cocos Plate moves a few inches closer to Costa Rica and, at the Middle America Trench, dives under the thicker Caribbean Plate, continuing to move not just across but also down toward the center of the earth.

This earth moving has created and reshaped the Costa Rican landscape. Sixty-five million years ago the subverting Cocos Plate uplifted the northwestern province of Guanacaste. Beginning only five million years ago, a mere tick in geological time, the Cocos Plate lifted the rest of the area now known as Costa Rica out of the water, making it one of the youngest geological formations in the world—the last country the gods made. Eventually this uplifting formed a permanent land bridge between North and South America. The compression caused by these two great movements formed the land's non-volcanic, backbone *cordilleras* (mountain ranges) called Tilarán, Aguacate, and Talamanca.

Forty miles east of these backbone cordilleras—and only a few million years ago—Costa Rica's volcanic activity began. Volcanism started late here relative to other volcanic areas like Japan, because the Cocos Plate ran into the Caribbean Plate such a short geologic time ago. After the two plates met

it took tens of millions of years for the subverted Cocos Plate to reach a depth where the earth's interior generated enough heat to melt its leading edge. The lighter elements of the then-liquid crust rose directly upwards and, under pressure, forced their way through ventilation shafts in the Caribbean Plate which at the surface became Costa Rica's arc of spectacular volcanoes.

The Costa Rican volcanoes Arenal, Poás, and Irazú are among the world's most active. Dormant for centuries, Volcán Arenal erupted violently in 1968, raining debris for miles. To this day thick lava flows slowly from its peak, and on dark nights threatening sparks reflect in the still waters of Lake Arenal on the flatlands below. Deep, green lakes fill the twin craters of Volcán Poás, so that every time it erupts, as it frequently does, mud and water shoot high into the air. In 1989, officials closed the park, fearing an eruption, and even today geyserlike blasts of sulfurous steam from one of the craters' lakes limit the park's hours. Volcán Irazú's nearly continuous eruption from 1963 to 1965 left its summit covered by dense, gray ash. This visually spectacular, almost lunar landscape sports eerie residents — a handful of cartoonish pioneer plants trying to reestablish the rain forest that was destroyed in the long volcanic explosion. These purple thistles and gigantic swaying ferns live with roving packs of wild horses, strange mustangs on this moonscape.

East of the phalanx of volcanoes lies the last portion of Costa Rica to emerge from the sea—the Atlantic Watershed. These coastal lowlands retain so much of the tropical moisture dumped on them that conventional roads are impractical, and an inland waterway through the continuous marsh serves as the only "freeway" from south to north.

The compression and uplift that made Costa Rica ends at the Atlantic shoreline, but other forces continue to alter the country's landscape. Lava flows and ash showers will transform the land for tens of thousands of years to come. The constant precipitation of the tropical climate continually reshapes the country's surface as well, eroding soils and growing great rain forests. In the last thousand years, however, nature has not wreaked the greatest change in Costa Rica; humanity has. Western colonization, conversion of forest to cropland by aboriginal and modern people, city-building, highway and rail construction, and revolution have created modern Costa Rica as much as mountain-building epochs of the past tempered the land.

Photographer's note

Before traveling to Costa Rica, I imagined it to be a place potent with beauty and passion. Once there, I found that it is such a place. Costa Rica is a gift to the senses, both cerebral and sensual, a feast for the traveler. During the year I spent there, I discovered an unspoiled country, preserved by the kindness of its people and exalted by the abundance of its landscape.

The images in this book can be seen everywhere in Costa Rica, around every corner. But one book of words and photographs cannot begin to capture the essence of the country. Knowing that, my ambition was to capture only elements of this special part of our world.

viii

I

Travels from the Interior:
the Costa Rican Landscape

*T*he Costa Rican national seal gives a revealing, stylized view of the country. In its foreground and background, sailing ships wait off the Caribbean and Pacific coasts. The sun sets over the Pacific, and between the oceans, the country itself sits as three huge volcanic cones surrounded by brush-covered lowlands. It's getting dark, and the only safe place in the picture is the nation's interior, flanked by these guardian volcanoes.

Costa Ricans saw the country's interior as a haven. Detesting the humid, insect-rich lowlands as unhealthy, the first European residents made the highlands their home instead of the unendurable tropics. Their attitude affected not only the country's depiction on the national crest, but also the Ticos' treatment of the landscape. Ticos, native Costa Ricans of Spanish ancestry, built the country from the inside out; roads, train tracks, and lines of communication resembled spokes radiating from a central hub, and still do today. For governmental convenience Costa Rica has seven provinces, but for practical considerations it has only two—the highlands and the outlands.

HIGHLANDS

Costa Rica's mountainous and volcanic arcs cradle between them an intermontane depression that Ticos call the Meseta Central, the "central plateau." The original Spanish colonists must have named it out of nostalgia for the great Castilian meseta of their homeland, because they could not have named it for any likeness between the two places. Bursts of ash from overtowering volcanoes make the rolling hills of the Meseta Central indefatigably fertile, little resembling the sparse, flat pasturelands of central Spain.

The continental divide runs through the Ochomogo Height, a rise between San José and Cartago that splits the Meseta into two halves, west and east. Rain in San José flows to the Pacific; rain in Cartago flows to the Caribbean. Flows of lava, ash, and mud from Irazú, Poás, Barva, and other volcanoes created the gracefully undulating floor of the Western Meseta Central. Irazú alone formed the Eastern Meseta. At times these flows blocked off rivers that drained the Meseta, forming temporary lakes that donated sediment to the area's rich alluvial soil. Eventually these rivers cut through the hardened lava flows and reached the sea. On the banks of the Rio Aguacaliente (Hot Water River), a trained eye can pick out volcanic rock layers whittled by the river as it tried to get to the Atlantic coast.

Climate

The Spanish settled in the Meseta Central because its climate resembled temperate Spain more than the hot, humid lands below. In this central part of the country, a mile above sea level, the temperature stays around 70°F. The humid tropical air that the Spanish so abhorred drops most of its moisture on the outer slopes of the mountains, making the Meseta one of the driest areas of Costa Rica. Although Ticos use the terms winter and summer, *invierno* and *verano*,

3

they do not correspond to the seasons of the Northern Hemisphere, but to the rainy and dry seasons of the tropics.

Between May and October the rainy season advances. When northeasterly trade winds from the Northern Hemisphere and southeasterly trade winds from the Southern Hemisphere meet and cancel each other out, the doldrums (low pressure areas) are created just off the Pacific coast, allowing moist, westerly winds to blow over Costa Rica. The westerlies make it over the relatively low Aguacate Mountains and dump their water on the floor of the Meseta, particularly on the western sides of the high volcanoes.

The dry season comes between November and April, simply because the doldrums move to the Southern Hemisphere and the easterlies from the Atlantic dominate. Even in the dry season, however, the sun heats up moist air on the central valley's floor; the air rises, cools, then drops its moisture in light afternoon showers on the volcanic slopes. When the rains come around March 20, Ticos speak of the *aguacero de los cafetaleros* (the coffee growers' shower), because the moisture opens the white flowers of coffee plants.

Agriculture

No meteorologist could manufacture a better climate than that of Costa Rica for growing coffee, the dominant cash crop in the Meseta; no agriculturalist could compound a better soil than the mineral-rich ash deposits of the Western Meseta. High organic content and excellent drainage make the valleys' soil perfect, not only for Arabica coffee plants but for a multitude of other agricultural products as well. The Eastern Meseta consists mainly of alluvial soils composed of silt and organic matter deposited by water left standing temporarily.

Fertile soil made the Meseta a favored area not only for the Spanish but also for the Indian peoples before them. The indigenous people practiced shifting cultivation, burning a section of the primary tropical, wet forest, farming for a spell, then moving on until secondary forest growth reclaimed the land. At any given time before Spanish exploration, cropland accounted for only a tiny part of the Meseta. Unlike the Indians, however, the Spanish did not plan merely to subsist on the land—they intended to make the land pay. As demand for agricultural production increased, colonial farmers razed more of the forest and decreased the amount of fallow time allowed each section of land, quickly converting much of the forest within a day's walk of Spanish towns to permanent cropland.

Before the 1800s, most Ticos worked common lands or rented plots. A minority of landowners ran small family farms, growing a mixture of subsistence and market crops. Hacienda-style farms never developed in the Meseta, simply because the unlanded labor force such large estates required did not exist. After coffee cultivation became popular in the 1840s, the Costa Rican government encouraged peasants to move away from the cities, carve plots out of the wilderness, and raise coffee for the motherland. Thousands of formerly landless peasants became small landholders, and more forest came under the axe.

With characteristic Tico generosity, Costa Rican farmers did not practice primogeniture, the giving of an entire family plot to the first-born male child, but instead divided family holdings among all their sons, and sometimes among their daughters as well. Within a few generations, this tradition atomized sizeable homesteads into discrete farms that could not support a family. Farmers had to rent plots to increase their production, labor on larger farms to get outside income, or move to the frontier.

Similar to many New World cultures, Ticos have traditionally solved problems of soil depletion, overpopulation, and land management by moving farther toward the uncultivated frontier, attempting to leave these problems behind them. In contrast to the United States, where settlers swept east to west, Tico farmers pushed the Costa Rican frontier outward from the Meseta Central in concentric rings. High-yield commercial products like coffee shoved subsistence-crop farmers to the edges of the Meseta, then up the sides of the volcanoes and down the fertile river valleys. Many vegetables sold in Tico markets today grow on the south slope of Irazú; the road from Cartago to the volcanic summit winds past fields of onions, cabbage, and potatoes.

These historical movements of Tico farmers are drawn plainly on the Costa Rican landscape. Permanent cropland covers almost the entire Meseta Central, but individual plots of cultivated land seem small. Coffee grows everywhere: within arm's reach of the road, within feet of a farmhouse door, on harrowing slopes, on seemingly inaccessible terraces. Costa Rica has no huge coffee *fincas* (plantations) like Honduras or Brazil. Small plots have as few as fifteen plants; larger ones may have a few hundred. To double the land's output and filter the harsh sun, farmers grow productive shade trees like banana and citrus among the coffee bushes.

Since the 1970s, when Costa Rican and world banks began promoting beef exportation as a means of paying off the country's considerable debt, cattle have become almost as ubiquitous as coffee. Farmers graze cattle on all unplanted fields, and ranchers have converted even marginal lands to pasture. This cattle craze has shoved subsistence crops even further to the outskirts of the Meseta and decreased the total area of land given to raising food for Ticos.

Despite the nearly complete conversion of wet forest to cropland, the undulating hills of the Meseta rage with flora. Unlike the quiltlike layout of fields in the American Midwest, the cropland here shares space with towering trees trying to reestablish the jungle among the plots. Palm trees stand abreast like privacy hedgerows, planted at the edges of the coffee groves to deter erosion. Hills are so deeply terraced they look like ziggurats. But even this ceaselessly florid aspect of the highlands has begun to change in recent years with the encroachment of cities and towns into the rural landscape.

Towns

Apart from San José, every settlement in the Meseta and the rest of Costa Rica can be classified as a town or village, not

a city. Although each town, particularly one of the original colonial centers, has a character of its own, the basic layout of each village never varies. A city square or plaza marks the town center. A market faces one side of the square, and a church faces another side. Within a block or two of the square, the commercial district dissolves into housing. On their outskirts, larger towns have stadiums and industrial parks. A school's location depends upon the town's age. In the older settlements, the school lies several blocks away from the square, but in newer ones it might face the square, as do the market and the church. Some of the newest villages have gone even farther by building not around a church and a square but around a school and a soccer field, reflecting the primacy of education and sports in modern Tico society.

In the Meseta with the metropolis of San José are Costa Rica's three other original colonial towns: Alajuela, Heredia, and Cartago. Lying directly northwest of San José, Alajuela, and, to a greater extent, Heredia have lost their town identities by their close association with the city; their commuters' lives center around San José. Meanwhile, the southeastern town of Cartago, by virtue of distance, has escaped a suburban fate and retained its distinct community life.

Broad-leaved mango trees provide shade for old men and dogs in Alajuela's town square, which features a statue of a drummer boy holding a torch—the national hero of Costa Rica. Juan Santamaría, a boy from a poor Alajuelan peasant family, perished setting North American invader William Walker's headquarters on fire. The townspeople, obviously

proud of their native son, turned the former jail into the Juan Santamaría Museum. In the shadow of Irazú and the colonial capital for three hundred years, Cartago's central square sports garden-filled cathedral ruins and a Byzantine church built in honor of Costa Rica's patron saint, La Negrita (The Black Madonna). The bells of this basílica ring over rows of kaleidoscopic-colored houses, painted in yellow, green, and red shades. Tall navy blue, purple, and beige iron fences front every house. Cartagans have made ornamental art from what is necessary for security.

Metropolis

Outlying towns influence their local regions, but Costa Rica has only one central place, one major urban area: San José. San José predominated over Cartago, Heredia, and Alajuela when it became the headquarters of the colonial tobacco industry in the late eighteenth century. After independence in 1821, Costa Rica's coffee empire built up around San José as well, ensuring the city's primacy in the modern era. Coffee barons planned and built the central city, but it has grown beyond their efforts spontaneously, with little planning, like most cities in developing countries.

Its setting alone places San José alongside the most beautiful cities in Latin America. The overgrown slopes of the surrounding mountains, visible from every vantage point, make San José seem an urban mirage in a rural utopia. Government buildings, business parks, museums, and urgent pedestrians intermingle with cafes, markets, and historical structures to create a continental yet distinctly regional atmosphere. The city has long since outgrown its old quarter, which has become a purely commercial district built around the Avenida Central, a long pedestrian market that begins at the city's most venerable building—the century-old National Theater.

Though dwarfed by surrounding high-rises, the National Theater dominates the central city by its spirit. Costa Ricans built it in a typically Tico act of will. A European diva touring Central America in 1890 refused to play Costa Rica for lack of a suitable venue. To obviate any repetition of this insufferable indignity, coffee growers placed a special tax on every bag of beans to build the National Theater. The money bought Belgian architects, Italian marble, and by 1897, a replica of the Paris Opera that became the centerpiece of Tico social life for decades. Recently renovated inside and out, the National Theater reflects the glory of its first days. Statues of European composers flank the entrance; musical instruments in plaster decorate the entry. The generous red velvet interior, with its rising boxes and balconies, conjures up images of La Scala. The coffee barons' desire to meet not merely local but global standards characterizes many past and present Costa Rican accomplishments.

By less direct methods, coffee built the rest of San José as well. Since 1950 the metropolis has grown from a population of 200,000, spread over an area of forty square kilometers, to a population of over one million, spread over an area of one thousand square kilometers. This astronomical population

9

rise occured not by reproductive increase but by immigration from rural areas. Residential expansion spurred the building of new hospitals and businesses away from the old quarter, the National University moved to the bedroom community of Heredia, and industrial parks relocated on cheaper land away from the center city.

Ticos forgot only one thing in their cityscape: parks. With the persistent view of the mountains, the need for green space could easily have slipped their minds. The builders of San José were saved from this oversight by a fluke: the old airport moved, leaving a fifteen-square-block expanse at the west side of the city. Wisely, the city did not pave the vacated land, but made a series of walking paths, soccer fields, and playgrounds called La Sabana. The Costa Rican Museum of Art moved into the old plane terminal. To help improve the next generation of Tico drivers, the city of San José even built a miniature city with traffic lights and stop signs, where children tool about in electric cars.

Naturally, San José's rapid growth and modernization has generated many problems familiar to the industrial world, such as pollution and suburban sprawl. Pollution, in reality a perennial problem, becomes visible only in the dry season. In the wet season, rains wash the smog from the sky; in the months without precipitation, the dirty air hangs as a miasma over the intermontane depression. Trapped by atmospheric inversion, which occurs when a blanket of cold air spanning the mountains prevents hot, polluted air in the Meseta from rising, the smog obscures the mountaintops by afternoon.

The usual villains, automobile and industrial fumes, mix with smoke from fires. Out of historical habit, Ticos burn everything—trash, tree clippings, and overgrown fields. From a high vantage point, plumes from a thousand little fires lit across the Meseta seem like columns supporting the mass of smog above.

Lacking the money for vertical housing projects, urban Ticos have chosen to spread horizontally. Because suburban sprawl moves not concentrically outward but ribbonlike instead, along roads, San José's metropolitan zone includes many smaller towns. It includes Heredia and threatens to engulf Alajuela and Cartago. Since 1950, greater San José has paved more than twelve thousand acres of coffee groves, rivaling in relative terms the orange tree destruction of Southern California during the same period. This loss of prime farmland, coupled with the fact that delivering services like electricity and water to a spread-out population costs much more than to a dense one, has put a drag on the Costa Rican economy.

Rails and Roads

Located in highlands away from the coasts, without a navigable river and surrounded by virtually impassable terrain, residents of the Meseta have struggled throughout their history with communication and transportation. Narrow, virtually imperceptible trails through the jungle provided avenues of transport for the Indians, but Spanish settlers wanted reliable roads to Nicaragua, the seat of

11

local government, and to both coasts. In 1601, one trail, ambitiously called the Camino Real (the True Way), attempted to provide clear passage to all three destinations. It wound down from Nicaragua through Nicoya and along the Pacific coast to Esparza, then up to the Meseta and back down to the Caribbean along the rugged banks of the Reventazón River. Tropical rains and steep terrain made travel excruciatingly slow, and, to make it worse, landslides and overgrowth often obscured the trail. In the 1700s, Ticos entered the colonial mule trade, which improved the flow of goods and information, but the Meseta still sat isolated from the world.

In the late 1800s, the need for a transport system that could handle the Meseta's coffee output reached a peak, and the Costa Rican government all but sold off the rest of the country to buy one set of rails from the Meseta Central to Port of Limón on the Atlantic coast. This track guided the famous "Jungle Train." Ultimately, events incidental to the actual construction—financial scheming, importation of labor, land giveaways, and money-raising projects—affected the country more drastically than the railroad itself. Later, with less ado, Ticos funded a similar rail line to Puntarenas. Completed around the turn of the century, these two lines provided the connection to both coasts that Costa Rica's mushrooming export economy demanded.

Today no one can experience the harrowing train ride along the steep banks of the Reventazón River, since the Jungle Train between the Meseta and the lowlands stopped running in 1991, 101 years after its inaugural journey. According to the contracts ruling its construction, a British firm ran the train until 1989. Knowing they would eventually have to give it up, the British let the rail system disintegrate, leaving Costa Ricans with a line of track ready to fall into the river. Alongside the remains of the great Jungle Train runs the newest addition to Costa Rican transport—an oil pipeline. It stands as an outcrop here and there, jutting from the surrounding jungle, sometimes running alongside the abandoned tracks, sometimes running away from them.

At the same time the country's rail network fell apart, the highway from San José to Limón, which traverses Braulio Carrillo National Park, replaced the train in economic importance and in the magnificence of its scenic route. Highways carry the vast majority of traffic and cargo in modern Costa Rica. Running from Nicaragua to Panama, the Pan-American Highway forms a trans-Isthmian axis linking many peripheral areas to San José. The Braulio Carrillo Highway from San José to Limón and the portion of the Pan-American Highway from San José to Puntarenas provide the transoceanic axis of transport, replacing railroads.

The roads may not meet international standards, however. In 1992, an American tourist wrote a letter to the English-language newspaper, the *Tico Times*, decrying the Pan-American Highway as "not a highway at all." It does have only two lanes and presents quite a hazard at night for cars when truck traffic gets heavier. Nonetheless, the Pan-American Highway remains serviceable, considering that it does not carry much traffic beyond central Costa Rica. All Costa Rican roads could improve, and they do suffer by comparison to North American highways, but Costa Rica did not set out to build a highway system that could support massive military troop movements as did the U.S., so should not be held to the same standards.

A more pressing problem with Costa Rican roads is that all roads lead to the Meseta Central. Very few roads lead elsewhere. This often creates illogical situations; for example, the cheapest way to conduct business between the Pacific coastal towns Puntarenas and Quepos entails shipping everything to San José and then shipping it back out again. Costa Rica's radial road network results in constantly overloaded exchanges in the Meseta itself and, more importantly, points to a problem caused by the traditional dominance of the central area. As modern Ticos certainly realize, they cannot merely send out lines of communication but must integrate lands beyond the Meseta into the country as a whole, reversing traditions set by their colonial foreparents.

OUTLANDS

Outside the Meseta Central, Costa Rica divides into four settled areas—Guanacaste and Nicoya to the northwest, the Atlantic Watershed to the east, and the Pacific Southwest. The Talamancan Mountains in the south comprise a fifth but mostly unsettled portion of the country.

Guanacaste and Nicoya

The Pacific Northwest, made up of the Nicoyan peninsula and the area above the Gulf of Nicoya called Guanacaste, formed beneath the sea 100,000,000 years ago. Within the last few million years, outpourings from the volcanoes of the Cordillera de Guanacaste have overlain parts of its ancient structures. Centuries of cattle farming, destroying the tropical dry forest that once covered the area, have left these geological formations exposed to the eye, the wind, and the rain. Where in other areas of Costa Rica distinctive vegetation characterizes different terrains, the Northwest seems carved out of the rock itself, changing color with the predominant minerals of each local area. Iron permeates the soil on the descent into Guanacaste from the Meseta, painting the hillsides a deep rust red. Around Liberia, prehistoric eruptions of rhyolite, a white volcanic rock, so dominate the landscape that Ticos call it the "white city."

Most of the Northwest looks like a hilly version of the Texas Panhandle, an impression fortified by grazing cattle. East of these plains rise the cordilleras Guanacaste and Tilarán, green and fertile, where some of the country's last remaining tropical cloud forest grows on the higher slopes. The cordilleras distinctly contrast with the much older water- and wind-worn hills of Nicoya. These ranges lie on the western edge of the Costa Rican landmass, their streams falling fast, steep, and violent to the Pacific. Waterfalls and rapids abound in the rivers of Guanacaste and on the entire Pacific coast. In the wet season, the Tempisque River,

15

running into the Gulf of Nicoya, carries so much water that it floods a wide area, depositing fertile soil on the plain in its retreat.

The Northwest's shoreline itself attracts most visitors, both Ticos and foreigners, to the area. On the peninsula's Pacific shore, the jagged land drops swiftly, creating narrow but spectacular beaches. The coastlines of the island-studded Gulf of Nicoya and the Santa Elena Bay slope much more shallowly to the beach, creating mangrove swamps and forests that stop just a few feet from the water. Most islands in the gulf are natural paradises, protected by law from human exploitation. Riders on the Punterenas ferry that crosses the Gulf of Nicoya get tantalizing glimpses of these islands on their way across the water. One island, San Lucas, housed one of Central America's most notorious penitentiaries until a few decades ago, when the government converted it into a prison for well-behaved inmates.

The seasons in Guanacaste and the Nicoyan peninsula correspond closely to the seasons in the Meseta Central, but the Northwest has a longer dry season. From December to May, when the doldrums move south and the easterlies reassert their domination, the bare plains of Guanacaste bake in the sun. The driest months of January, February, and March witness polar winds arriving in the Northwest as hot dry papagayos, tearing up whatever dirt the rains left and turning Guanacaste into a dust bowl.

For four hundred years, the inhabitants of Guanacaste have raised cattle. The Brahmin grazing there today on insuf-

ficient-looking bits of grass positively did not descend from those earliest herds of Spanish longhorns, however. Traditionally, ranchers grazed their cattle in the lowlands during the wet season and in the dry season moved them up into the hills of the cordilleras Guanacaste or Tilarán. Ironically, this mimicked the migration pattern of many animals in the dry forest—a habitat that ranching all but destroyed. Property fences eventually stopped upland grazing, so ranchers turned the entire plains of Guanacaste from dry forest into pasture to increase the amount of grass available to their herds.

In other parts of Costa Rica, the rise of the beef-export industry prompted large-scale conversion of forest to pastureland. But in Guanacaste, where savanna expansion could not be carried much further, the ranchers chose to intensify their ranching techniques. They imported hearty African grasses for grazing, then fattened cattle on imported grains. These measures have decreased the need for more pastureland, slowing habitat destruction for the moment, and producing a higher quality meat as well.

Atlantic Watershed

Just to the east of the Cordillera de Guanacaste lies the Atlantic Watershed, so named because all the area's plentiful rain flows to the Atlantic. This triangular region, bordered by Nicaragua, the Atlantic coast, and the mountains, takes up more land mass than any other area in Costa Rica. Barely lifted above sea level, it slopes gently to the shore, so the rivers run slow and deep and the land stays almost water-

17

logged. Once covered by wet forest adapted to the moist environment, the area now supports logging and various agricultural industries. Whatever the enterprise, it must survive a constantly rainy climate.

Most of the rain comes in with the easterly trade winds, which blow east to west because the earth turns to the east. The earth moves through the atmosphere much as a swimmer moves through water—the swimmer drags some water with her, but most of it remains fixed as she moves swiftly by. The atmosphere's reluctance to move manifests itself as a constant wind that earthbound people feel as an easterly breeze, even though we are the ones rushing by. Near the equator, where the earth moves fastest, easterlies dominate other forces. As these trade winds scud over the Caribbean toward the Atlantic coast of Costa Rica, they gather moisture off the surface of the sea. Rising a bit when they encounter the Costa Rican landmass, the winds drop their water on Costa Rica's Atlantic Watershed.

The Watershed region has no real seasons—unless wet, wetter, and wettest qualify. Wettest occurs from January through March when the polar winds reach Costa Rica, as close to the equator as they get. Wet occurs from June to October when the doldrums move north and weaken the rain-bearing trade winds. Wetter covers the rest of the year.

Early Spanish settlers despised the Atlantic Watershed. Few activities could flourish in such a sodden climate, and the lowlands encouraged insect-borne diseases, unhealthy to any human population without modern medical treatments. The Spanish left the area unsettled, and by tradition the Ticos stayed away also, leaving it sparsely populated until a century ago, when they decided they needed a railroad to the coast. Ticos had no cash, so they bought the rails with land in the late 1880s. Not surprisingly, they gave away the presumedly worthless lowlands to American rail builders who knew they could cultivate bananas there, since those plants craved abundant water, heat, and rich soil. The Americans imported black Jamaican laborers and turned the hinterlands of Limón into a huge banana plantation, making Costa Rica the first banana-exporting country in Central America.

The successful banana industry did not last long. In the 1930s, Panama plant disease destroyed the entire plantation, and the company moved to the Pacific coast. In its wake, it left acres of depleted soil and a huge, now-idle labor force. To survive, the laborers resumed subsistence farming, raising cattle, logging a little, living off the shore, and revivifying the insignificant colonial cocoa industry. Since the 1930s, banana strains resistant to Panama disease have allowed rejuvenation of the old plantations. At present, much of the area around Limón has turned back to banana cultivation.

When the banana industry returned to the Atlantic Watershed, however, it found much of the land stripped of nutrients needed to support the new banana trees. So the American banana giant, United Brands (formerly United Fruit), imported a plant able to grow in thin soil—the African oil palm. Unlike bananas, oil palms don't make much money. They do make food for Ticos, though: the fibrous pulp around

the palm-fruit seed contains an edible oil widely used in Costa Rica. Although growers hoped to expand palm oil into an export industry, in the long run the domestic market strengthened the country's economy more than the export sales would have. Unfortunately, in the 1960s and 1970s, the World Bank, trying to predict the next revolution in export agriculture, encouraged farmers in every developing country to grow oil palms. The international market, now glutted, looks bleak.

Limón, the port city for the banana and coffee industries and the cultural center for the black population, resembles a Caribbean town more than a Costa Rican one. The Palm Promenade and the botanicals of Parque Vargas provide a break from Limón's boomtown-gone-bust atmosphere. Built just over a century ago, the city became a cosmopolitan port and a company town for thousands of Jamaican workers. After Panama disease reshaped the area's labor needs, the town went to seed. Today Limón seems only half rebuilt. Though it is still an important docking area, modern port facilities nine miles to the north in Moín handle the largest vessels.

In the Meseta Central, the people came first and transportation followed. In the Atlantic Watershed, the reverse occurred—rails, roads, and canals provided easy access to undeveloped areas, then populations followed in their wake. Towns rose up beside the tracks of the Jungle Train, and more recently along the new road to Limón. North of the banana zone, the land stays too wet to build roads, so water-

ways provide the only means of transport. Inhabitants have always traveled by boat on the navigable tributaries of the San Juan River and in the coastal estuaries. In 1974, Ticos connected these various waterways by dredging passages between hundreds of coastal lagoons, creating a continuous inland canal that runs from Moín to Tortuguero. Sloths, snakes, and resplendent birds overlook the waterway from treetops as it transports logs from northern mills to Limón. Eco-tourists boat along the shore to watch thousands of female Atlantic green turtles that come only to this black beach, trundling out of the sea in the dead of night to lay their eggs in an annual event called the *arribada* (arrival).

Talamancas

The largest wilderness in Costa Rica, the Talamancan Mountains rise sharply between the southern Atlantic and Pacific lowlands. Created about fifty million years ago by compression, they contain no volcanoes. They are rugged nonetheless. Colonial Ticos viewed most areas outside the Meseta as unfriendly, but the Talamancas proved to be unfriendliest. Repeated attempts to colonize the area resulted in bloody, epic failure. Containing no suitable farmland, the area today plays a crucial role as a forested watershed. No towns, roads, or industries penetrate these forests. The region's weather also makes human settlement difficult. Climate varies with altitude in the Talamancas; warm rain pelts the lower ranges, while dry winds bring temperatures below freezing on Costa Rica's highest peak, Mount Chirripó.

Pacific Southwest

From the Talamancas, the land declines to the Pacific through a series of plateaus, finally reaching the area's seaward-most land mass, the Osa Peninsula. Between the Talamancas and the coastal Costeña Mountains lie the General and Coto Brus intermontane depressions, both of which held lakes millions of years ago. Seaward of the Costeñas lie two lower-altitude depressions, the Térraba and the Coto Colorado. At the verge of the sea, these valleys give way to the hills of the Osa and Burica peninsulas. A rocky finger into the Pacific, the Osa Peninsula shelters the Golfo Dulce (Sweet Gulf), one of the calmest harbors along the stormy Pacific coastline.

The rivers of the Southwest come swift and dangerous, like those of Guanacaste. Ticos wisely exploit these natural sources of energy, building hydroelectric plants on their courses that produce ninety-eight percent of the electricity used in the nation. The runoff from the General and Coto Brus valleys feeds the great Diquis River, which cuts through the Costeña mountains and meets the Pacific in a wide, fan-like delta north of the Osa Peninsula. The less tumultuous Coto Colorado River, which drains the valley of the same name, has created a large, fertile floodplain, now exploited for agriculture.

The landscape of the Southwest varies widely with altitude and soil; everything from coffee to coconuts can thrive in its varied terrains. The General Valley has poor, nonvolcanic soil, but this drawback did not discourage pioneers. Shoved out of the Meseta by early twentieth-century coffee expansion, subsistence farmers colonized the area around San Isidro, initially growing food crops such as rice, beans, and corn for the home market. Today, the region's farmers predominantly raise cattle for export, making pasture of most of the upper valley. Low-grade coffee for the home market and sugar cane also grow here. Since cane must be moved to processing plants within hours of harvest, before the sugar degrades, the industry profits from having relatively good roads around San Isidro.

Historically, farmers from the General Valley spilled over into the adjacent Coto Brus Valley and began raising cash crops of their own. The Chiriqui volcano in Panama had showered the Coto Brus valley with volcanic ash, and the new arrivals quickly discovered that this mineral-rich soil, combined with the area's consistent dry season, provided perfect conditions for growing high-grade Arabica coffee. Today, the Coto Brus Valley produces more Arabica beans than any Costa Rican area outside the Meseta.

In upper valleys, export crops followed large-scale colonization, but the opposite held true in lower valleys. After Panama disease wiped out its Atlantic-side coffee plantations in the 1930s, United Brands moved to the Pacific. The company quickly developed the Térraba and Coto Colorado valleys for banana production. Company engineers installed drainage ditches to control the flooding of the Diquis, putting much more land under cultivation than could have been done without such enormous capital investment. After

the 1950s, agricultural colonists entered the area in force, cultivating mixed crops, particularly rice, in the Coto Colorado valley. United Brands pulled out of the area in 1985 when oil palms supplanted the banana groves.

Despite the geographic similarity between the Meseta Central and the Southwest plateaus, difficult passage made the plateaus the last highland area colonized. The Pan American Highway, which has since solved the transport problem, traces the pioneers' difficult route out of Cartago, cutting across the Talamancas. From the floor of the Meseta, the road rises a mile to traverse cloud forests. Then, in the most spectacular drive in the country, it plummets one-and-a-half miles down to the General Valley floor. The highway continues down the middle of the General, follows the Diquis River through the Costeña Mountains, then skirts the seaward side of that range into Panama.

Before reaching San Isidro, the highway passes a colossal statue of Jesus with a halo of green grass growing in a semi-circle around the black rock outcropping behind him. Hands posed in a benediction, he overlooks the valley from a summit. San Isidro sits squeezed into the northwest corner of the large oblong General depression. Seemingly an unsuitable location for a central town, this spot had a historical advantage because it provided a flat settlement site for the first pioneers. San Isidro sprawls irregularly across the valley floor, roads starting in all directions from its typical church-and-square center; the grid plan survives only a few blocks before it breaks up. Mainly a rural service center, the town supports some light industry, banks, and schools.

Italian immigrants founded the main town of the Coto Brus Valley in the 1950s. They built San Vito close to the planned route of the Pan American Highway, but the road skipped the valley altogether in construction, so most of the town's founders moved away. The steep road to San Vito passes through a fantastic wilderness and continues into a modern town of Italian speakers and Italian restaurants.

At the base of the Costeña Mountains, United Brands constructed Golfito from the ground up as a port facility for its Pacific plantations. Lying on a thin strip of coast surrounded by wooded cliffs, the town looks across the Golfo Dulce toward the Osa Peninsula. Before the banana company moved out, Golfito bustled—one-third port, one-third company town, one-third luxury residence for North American executives. Today, the company has gone, and under the new order only the port remains fully functional, overlooked rather oddly by high-rent housing and overgrown golf courses.

24

II

Pre-Columbian Costa Rica

Costa Rican Indians, long seen as a group that simply reacted to the great northern and southern cultures of Mesoamerica and Peru, have recently come into their own, as cultural historians have realized that their Pre-Columbian ancestors had a distinct culture. Naturally, these early peoples received cultural and technological imports from their more advanced neighbors. In their most important aspects, however, Costa Rican Pre-Columbian cultures developed independently.

In theory, all Amerindians descend from nomadic bands of Mongoloids who migrated from Siberia to Alaska 40,000 to 10,000 years ago, using a temporary land bridge across the Bering Strait. Similarly, all South American Indians come from groups that crossed Central America, the land bridge between North and South America. Eventually, South American hunter-gatherers dominated northern groups in the settling of Costa Rica, because their experience in the rain forests of Colombia and Ecuador gave them an advantage in the forested Costa Rican terrain. Around 5000 B.C., a shore-area lifestyle able to support many more people than simple hunting and gathering spread from Ecuador to Costa Rica. Between 1500 B.C. and A.D. 1, an even more efficient agricultural lifestyle, again from Ecuador, replaced this shore culture. The new agriculturists used slash-and-burn techniques to cultivate maize and root crops like cassava, a starchy tuberous plant from which Amerindians made bread.

By A.D. 1, Costa Rican Indians had separated into three regional groups based on the South American forest culture.

Those in the southwest Diquis region had ties to the adjacent section of Panama; those in the northwest Nicoya area had ties to the adjacent section of Nicaragua; those in the remainder of the country, the Central Highlands and Atlantic Watershed regions, did not range beyond modern Costa Rican borders.

Tribes in all three areas had feudal social structures based on male lineage. (A Nicoyan tribe ruled by a democratically elected town council and a large Atlantic Watershed tribe with female chiefs provide the exceptions to this rule.) Generally, each tribe had a single male ruler, the cacique, who upon death passed the sacred office to his son. Family clans making up the tribe each had their own cacique, who acted as a vassal to the great cacique, fighting for him in battle and giving him tribute in peacetime. Below each vassal served warriors and a lower class, which consisted of tribe members or of slaves captured from other tribes. Tribal women bore children and worked the fields, and in some tribes they fought in battle alongside men.

The great cacique lived in a structure at the center of each town. Some towns had walls for defense, and easily defendable stone roads led to the cacique's house. Amerindians built no housing structures of stone, however, instead using leaves and grasses, which kept out the constant rain better than stone could. The steeply raked grass roof of each dwelling peaked at a chimney hole, which sometimes had a pot sitting on top to keep the rain out. Each clan lived in a separate dwelling that held from twenty-five to four hundred people.

Village populations numbered from a few hundred to more than a thousand.

The largest community in the Atlantic Watershed, El Guayabo, had aqueducts that guided water from several area springs. Stairs and stone walkways crisscrossed its compound. Seventeen separate communities resided in the El Guayabo complex. Miles-long and yards-wide cobblestone paths connected each community to others nearby.

All three regional cultures evolved non-farming settlements that performed specialized functions for the farming communities that supported them. The Diquis Indians, like medieval Europeans, built centralized fort towns containing up to sixteen hundred individuals, protecting smaller agricultural villages surrounding them. In Nicoya, some communities exclusively manufactured a purple dye from seashells and traded it. In the Atlantic Watershed and Diquis, artisans carved ritualistic stone statues.

In each tribe, the shaman or medicine man held the next most powerful position, after the cacique. Tribal shamans presided over a nature religion that originated in South America. The religion personified and assigned a gender to all things living and unliving. The sun, a male, stood as principal deity; the female earth stood below him. Bird gods had the freedom to fly among three cosmic realms—the underworld, the earth, and the heavens. The jaguar god guarded the underworld, as the alligator god ruled the earth. Bat gods were revered, because one origin myth told of how bat guano fertilized the first corn, from which humans came.

In another origin myth, humans came from monkeys, so monkey gods also had a place in Pre-Columbian worship.

The rites of this nature-based religion occurred on a daily and a monthly schedule. The first animate thing seen each morning ruled an individual for that day, and other omens influenced daily life. A shaman cupped small talismans called sukia stones in his hands, blowing on them, to make predictions about future or far-off events. Presumably, he would concentrate on the concerns of his farmer-hunter congregation, such as inclement weather and the timing of animal migrations. Aside from his duties as a clairvoyant, a medicine man oversaw a large temple with idols of gold, stone, wood, and clay, where the religion's strong preoccupation with death played out in gruesome sacrificial rites. In its most important religious practice, a tribe would make a human sacrifice to the gods in every lunar cycle. The importance of decapitation in this ceremony bred a trophy-head cult, where the heads of victims, or carved representations, became prized signs of status.

While nature religions remained pure in Diquis and Talamanca, around A.D. 500 a fertility cult moved into Nicoya and the Atlantic Watershed from the north. The new religion centered around phallic devices and drunken, orgiastic rites. Rooted in society more than nature, the phallic cult converted all the nature-based deities—birds, crocodiles, snakes, jaguars, and monkeys—into fertility gods.

The primary religious site in the Atlantic Watershed for this newer religion was Las Mercedes. Its walled complex

centered around a raised, circular temple guarded by four six-foot-tall, stone statues of human gods. Habitations outside the compound probably housed shamans, their families, and attendants. Las Mercedes served as a center for the old trophy-head cult, which had apparently survived as a part of the dominant fertility cult.

Influenced by their religion's obsession with death, Costa Rican Indians developed elaborate secondary burial customs. The Amerindians wrapped the newly dead in bark and stored them in the jungle for a year. They then retrieved the remains and buried them in stone-lined graves, which guarded against the effects of constantly wet ground on corpses. Artifacts placed in the graves (pots, gold, jade, stone plates for the ceremonial grinding of corn) ensured that the dead would receive the benefits of their status in the afterlife. Large stone or wood entablatures covered the graves of the truly revered.

Trade played such an important role in the life of Costa Rican Indians that when Columbus put anchor down outside the place now home to modern-day Limón, natives swam to his ships carrying goods for barter: clothing, arms, and gold pendants. Sophisticated networks of exchange, run by a class of merchants, crisscrossed the land, the inland waterways, and both coastlines. Serving mainly the elite, these merchants traded pigs, salt, cacao, cloth, gold-work, and slaves. Arti–facts from other cultures usually lost their context during transportation, and in any case, the Amerindian elite, as the elite of all times and places, did not attach functional significance or meaning to these new trade goods, but only wanted

them for the status they conferred.

Significant cultural and technological exchanges occurred less frequently than the activity of these trade networks suggests. The transmission of religious ideas, mortuary practices, agricultural techniques, habitation styles, and political organization occurred mostly by diffusion, a slow process in which a practice or lifestyle passes down the line from community to community. Cultural practices sometimes spread by immigration, as well, but never by simple trade.

Ecuadorian Indians ran a sporadic, marine trade network up and down the Pacific coast. Their habitual use of safe ports around the Osa peninsula and in the Bay of Nicoya ensured that many types of South American ceramics and other products reached Costa Rica shores. Columbian and Amazonian Indians plied similar trade routes in the Caribbean and along the San Juan River, which now forms the border between Nicaragua and Costa Rica. These traders brought South American and Antillean influences to the Costa Rican Atlantic Watershed and Central Highland areas.

The land-based trade networks that crisscrossed Costa Rica and all of Central America covered much less territory, 150 miles at the most, so long-distance exchanges over land obviously had to involve a series of overlapping systems. Called down-the-line networks, these systems exchanged goods and cultures at walking speed, at best. Many exchanges took years or decades to complete.

Around 1500 B.C., Pacific trade vessels brought maize cultivation from Mesoamerica to Ecuador. From there, maize

Costa Rican Indians, though permanently settled, created no urban centers. Gifted stonecutters, they built no monumental architecture or stone structures of any kind; fierce and frequent warriors, they never engaged in empire-building conquests. Unmolested by the Spanish, they might have done all these things in time. Strangely, though, Costa Rica's fertile soil, wet climate, and peculiarities of social structure retarded such advances, or made them unnecessary. 🏛 Contrary to common sense, the areas of the first great civilizations, such as Egypt, were ripe for empire-building not because they contained the most fertile land in the world, but because barren wastelands surrounded a fertile core area. In Egypt, the Sahara borders the Nile valley on the west, and the Arabian desert borders it on the east. Likewise, desert and dry grassland surround the fertile region of modern-day Mexico City, the center of the Aztec and Mayan empires. In both of these areas, strong rulers could hold sway over a large number of weak citizens because the weak had nowhere to go. Costa Rica contains no wastelands, and although the highland valleys are most fertile, the land remains arable throughout the country, providing a safety valve for oppressed groups. Enormous tracts of this productive land remained unoccupied up to the time of contact with the Spanish. If attacked, a group could simply migrate instead of submit. 🏛 Although it is difficult to picture medieval French wheat farmers pulling up roots and

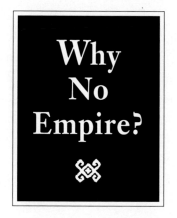

Why No Empire?

moving on to the the next province, the slash-and-burn agricultural methods of the Costa Rican Indians actually required that populations move occasionally. Native populations throughout Central America and northern South America farmed by cutting down sections of the once ubiquitous rain forest and burning the debris, a slash-and-burn process that simultaneously cleared a field and fertilized it. Belying the luxuriant-looking plant-life it supports, rain forest soil contains few nutrients and little mulch, so a clearing only remained fertile for five years. After tapping out a plot, the farmers had to move on. This emigration, built into the lifestyle of Costa Rican Indians, provided a mechanism for avoiding domination. 🏛 Costa Rican Indians were not forced together through conquest, but they also failed to come together through cooperation. While slash-and-burn agriculture uses some community labor to clear the forest and to harvest, it does not even approach the organization demanded for intensive agriculture. For instance, in large-scale cultivation of maize, Mesoamerican cousins to the north terraced the land to make fields, constructed irrigation systems, carefully coordinated the growing seasons, and most importantly, controlled the distribution of the food produced. Costa Rican slash-and-burn did not require that large groups of people work together. 🏛 In large-scale agriculture, distribution is the key to civilization and power. Mesoamerican chiefs made

31

decisions about who got food and who didn't. Because of the amount of food involved and the number of people fed, controlling distribution gave the chiefs power they could not have dreamed of in simple village society. They could then use this power and the work force at their disposal to erect monuments, build cities, direct wars of conquest, and do other things associated with advanced societies. In Costa Rica, large-scale maize production began in the Diquis area only eight hundred years before the Spanish conquest—hardly enough time for native communities to reach this level of social organization. 🏛 Intensive cultivation of maize caught on late in Costa Rica partly because it rained too much to store the grain year-round. Unlike maize, root crops like cassava don't need special storage; they can be left in the ground until needed, sometimes for years. Until A.D. 700, Costa Rican Indians grew a mixture of maize and easy-to-store root crops, supplementing these carbohydrates with protein from hunting or fishing. In particularly fertile areas like river valleys or highland plains, this lifestyle supported a fairly dense population. Only after they began the intensive cultivation of maize did these groups grow dense enough to support special-ization and a powerful ruling class. Increasing population density also forced Costa Rican Indians to compete for a limited amount of resources. Though most groups react to such pressure by conquering their neighbors or by initiating cooperative societies, Costa Rican Indians reduced population pressure by waging bloody intertribal wars. 🏛 Nature itself reacted to the carnage. In his explorations of the Diquis

area, Vasquez de Coronado, the most famous of the conquis-tadors, reported that "immediately [when] a war cry pierced the air, a flock of buzzards would gather large enough to obscure the sun." The warfare made entire tribes extinct. Fires set in battles raged for days, destroying so much of the southwest rain forest that they created, or at least expanded, the Buenos Aires plains. 🏛 This astonishing culture of destruction originated at the level of the tribal village, where a warrior society served a rational, though still violent, purpose. Since aboriginal Costa Ricans could not mate with members of their own tribe, men attacked another village and captured its women. They also raided neighboring groups to obtain victims for religious sacrifices to the moon and to capture slaves for their chiefs. On a small scale, these aggressive traditions decreased competition for common resources and prevented inbreeding. 🏛 To control an area larger than a village, most societies had to change their means of production and their methods of social organization. But Costa Rica's fertile soil allowed the Diquis and Central Highland Indians to support large populations by expanding tribal agriculture in scale. Alongside tribal agriculture, the Amerindians expanded the tribal warrior culture until it reached a catastrophically large scale. Even after the advent of intensive maize agriculture, these Amerindians continued their warlike behavior with disastrous results. And such patterns of genocidal warfare obviated the possibility of conquest or cooperation in Costa Rica, and combined with climate and geography to slow the formation of formal

32

civilization. Then again, perhaps the local Amerindians had no use for urban zones or concentrations of power that would have placed them in the ranks of advanced societies. At the time of European contact, the Amerindians numbered 500,000, a dense population for a country the size of West Virginia. Natives excelled in the so-called small arts of jade-, gold- and stonework, their societies supporting separate communities for artists, farmers, warriors, and leaders. If urbanity is the litmus test for civilization, consider this: in the Diquis area, the leaders lived not with the warriors as one might imagine, but with the artists. How urbane can you get?

cultivation spread by land to Costa Rica. Although the cultivation of corn that began in Mexico from 6000 B.C. to 5000 B.C. belonged to a seed-based agricultural system, the tropical forest culture that spread to most of Costa Rica grew corn through vegetable agriculture. Practitioners of vegetable agriculture had to supplement their diet with animal protein, since they mainly ate starch, while seed agriculturalists acquired enough protein from seeds to form sedentary societies. But vegetable cultivators had to work less hard, and did not need to organize planting times or figure out how to fertilize a field.

Vegetable agriculturalists did not deplete the soil as much as seed growers, since they never removed and replanted the seeds of the plants they ate. They ate the starchy part of the plants instead, and let another fruit or tuber grow in its place. They did not trouble with harvest times either, for the tubers generally kept in the ground until the people were ready to eat them. Along with corn, Atlantic Watershed Indians cultivated cacao and the peach-plum, both South American cultivants.

Corn came from Ecuador, and so did pottery to store it. The first ceramic tradition on the American continent developed around 3000 B.C. on the Ecuadorian coast in a region archaeologists term the Intermediate Area (including modern-day Ecuador, northern Colombia, western Venezuela, Panama, Costa Rica and eastern Nicaragua). These early American ceramics bear a striking resemblance to pottery of the ancient Japanese "Jomon" culture. Some archaeologists write this off as a coincidence, arguing that anyone could have come up with the simple, geometric designs. Others hypothesize that the counter-clockwise Japanese currents swept to the Ecuadorian shore a seaborne Jomon fisher who knew pot-making. Fantastic as the latter theory may sound, it has earned respect in archaeological circles. Regardless of the origin of their designs, Jomon-like ceramics spread from Ecuador throughout the Intermediate Area, including Costa Rica, and may have spread to Mesoamerica and Peru, where the earliest pottery traditions begin much later than 3000 B.C.

Naturally, local potters developed styles of their own, while incorporating elements of foreign ceramics. Though long-distance trade networks never transported mass quantities of ceramics, styles and techniques did travel, either through the incidental travel of an original piece or through the down-the-line trade of copies. Ecuadorian merchant mariners who found the Gulf of Nicoya to be a natural haven from Pacific squalls brought many goods, including ceramics, to the Amerindians of that region.

Around 0 B.C., the Nicoyans received from these traders some examples of Ecuadorian Chorrera-style pottery. The bold coloring and varied animal shapes of the Chorrera style inspired Nicoyan artists to produce similar wares. The resulting experimentations produced arguably the greatest pottery tradition in the New World: Nicoyan polychrome ceramics. Traders carried Nicoyan polychromes throughout Costa Rica and beyond. Nicoyan potters used realism and

34

humor to create an exquisite pottery tradition. In pots that are preserved today, squatting monkeys holding their heads in their hands make pitchers; water pours out of their laughing mouths. Inventive and original, the potters of Nicoya remained independent of any dogmatic artistic tradition, unlike the painters of ancient Egypt or the sculptors of Diquis. And the Amerindians of the Atlantic Watershed so valued Nicoyan polychrome that they buried it with their dead.

Ceramic work flourished throughout all three regions along with many other so called "small arts." Jade work was introduced to the West not by contact with China but by its conquest of the New World. Jade and greenstone carving abounded in Costa Rica from 300 B.C. to A.D. 700, but virtually no jade artifacts exist in Nicaragua to the north or in Panama to the south. At the same time, however, geologists can find no jade mine in the country and no evidence that one ever existed. This paradox does not distract from the rich native jade tradition. Costa Rican jade resembles Olmec-style samples from Mesoamerica. Apparently, a few pieces of Olmec jade pieces got to Costa Rica through down-the-line trading networks. Costa Rican Indians took to the art form and fostered jade artisanship.

Jade artifacts mainly take the form of axe-head pendants. Native Costa Ricans cleared the forest with axes made of celts (stone axe heads), in slash-and-burn agriculture. Because of their importance to life, and because, in use, they made a sound like lightning, the companion of life-giving rain, axes became talismans. Artisans took actual or ceremonial celts as bases for their sculptures. Leaving untouched the smooth cutting end of the celt, they carved the figure of a god in the end that would have been lashed to a branch had the celt served as an axe. The incredibly durable jade celts served as symbols of power, signs of a valid lineage, and became valuable trade items for their elite owners. Jade working stopped in the region by A.D.1000, possibly because Amerindian groups switched their artistic attention to gold.

The South American technique of gold-working made its way up the Caribbean coast only as far as Costa Rica, reaching the area in A.D. 500. Mesoamerican cultures to the north learned the art from Costa Rican Indians, not from the original source. The artisan gold tradition used complex manufacturing techniques, such as polishing the gold with plant-derived acid washes and using lost-wax casting, which conserved the resource by creating thinner pieces. In the lost-wax method, the artisan placed a minute layer of wax between two tightly fitted molds. He or she then poured molten gold into the space, melting and replacing the wax. Once separated, the molds revealed an ornament in the shape of the molds and as thin as the original wax layer. The natives of Diquis and the Atlantic Watershed excelled in this metallurgy, which became a huge export up and down both coasts. Their artisans made finely crafted figures—bats, frogs, and bells among them—for rituals, trade, status symbols, and burial tokens for high-ranking dead. Since Costa Rican gold did not concentrate in mines, but rather ran down rivers, Diquis tribes located their riverside villages in good spots for gold washing.

36

The most striking and enigmatic of all Costa Rican pre-Columbian art comes from the Diquis lowlands, where for many centuries the natives produced huge stone spheres. From an artisan culture that carved stylized human figures, the sculptors also made huge stone spheres of igneous rock. With the largest reaching twenty feet in circumference and weighing up to sixteen tons, these rocks probably served as cult symbols. Arranged in lines and arcs, they may have had astronomical meaning. The enormous amounts of labor and artistic talent required to transport rock from the mountains and carve the spheres imply a cultural stability not observed by the Spanish, who told only of Diquis bellicosity. The Central American Stonehenge, the true purpose of the Diquis balls remains one of the earth's greatest prehistorical mysteries, along with the heads of Easter Island. Today, smaller Diquis balls can be glimpsed all over Costa Rica, in fields and in private residences. Sometimes the sculptures sit in front of homes or buildings, with rainbows painted on the sides of the balls facing the street and passers-by.

No one is certain of the cultural origins of the Diquis creations. It is clear that by A.D. 1000, Costa Rican Indians began to feel a strong Mesoamerican influence. In that era, several tribes from the dissolving Mayan empire migrated south into Guanacaste, displacing the resident natives and bringing their own culture with them. At contact, a tribe of cannibalistic Mesoamerican tribute collectors lived around Limón—presaging a greater penetration of the area by Aztecs.

Amerindians of all three areas shared a love of war, which might explain why Costa Rican Indians never suffered a large invasion from northern or southern empires. Tragically, the local bellicosity also ensured demise at the hands of the war-loving Spanish. In the early phases of conquest, groups of Amerindians actually enlisted the Spanish to help them destroy their enemies. But when Spanish people began to colonize, the remaining tribes put up prolonged resistance, so the Spanish annihilated most, assimilated some, and drove the rest into remote areas, where the last five tribes of Costa Rica exist today. The Bribri and the Cabecarés live on the Atlantic slope of the Talamancan Mountains, the Borucas and the Térrabas live on the Pacific slope, and the Guatusos inhabit obscure sections of northern Costa Rican jungle.

38

Archaeologists attempt to reconstruct a dead society from its material remains, and when possible, interpret their finds in the light of firsthand descriptions of the culture. Unfortunately, sixteenth-century Spaniards recorded few, if any, details of native life, generally restricting their interest in Costa Rican Indians to a "soul and gold count"—how many natives they converted and how much loot they collected from them. Analogies with existing parallel cultures, another tool of the archaeologist, do not apply as well in Spanish America as in other areas of the world because the genocidal destruction wreaked by the Spanish conquest disturbed native society too much to assume that any ancient practices continue unchanged in modern Amerindian villages. As a result, archaeologists only timidly assume that surviving cultures relate to pre-contact cultures. The trouble with Costa Rican archaeology, therefore, is in its necessary and almost exclusive reliance on material remains. 🏛 In Costa Rica, merely excavating useful physical remains has proven difficult. Organic material like bones, food remnants, and wood rarely survives in the tropical damp, leaving archaeologists with imperishables—ceramics, gold, jade, and stone—which unfortunately have value beyond archaeological significance. Collectors, most from outside Latin America, have created a demand for ancient artwork satisfied by local

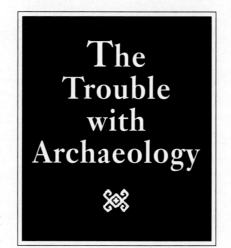

The Trouble with Archaeology

huaqueros or grave-robbers. Uncontrolled excavations by *huaqueros* and collectors from the nineteenth century to the present have ruined a majority of native sites and prevented Costa Rican archaeology from progressing beyond a primitive state. 🏛 Archaeologists can't make much use of artifacts found in collections or those found in a site disturbed by *huaqueros*. Only remains found in context can provide archaeologists pieces to the puzzle of an ancient society. A pot shaped like a human head found in a grave might mean that the culture provided a vessel for the soul or a companion in the afterlife. The same pot found in a living area may signify that it served in ritual ceremonies. A head-shaped pot outside a definite context gives no basis for speculation. 🏛 Hobbled by these various setbacks, Costa Rican archaeologists took until the 1970s to complete the classification phase of their science, wherein they defined the date and location of manufacture, the area of distribution, and the general use of most common artifacts. Only with this knowledge in hand could archaeologists approach the goal of archaeology—the description of ancient Costa Rican societies. 🏛 Even now, scholars face difficulties in determining how much of Costa Rican Indian society developed by internal mechanisms and how much grew under foreign influences. Archaeologists can always hold up physical proof of outside

39

contact (a gold bell from Mesoamerica found in a Costa Rican grave, for example), so tend to give too much weight to external influence. Proving the reverse—that a society developed by internal mechanisms—is not so simple. 🏛 Cultures under foreign influence tend to change sporadically or suddenly, so only by demonstrating that a culture changed continuously, without such leaps and bounds, can archaeologists eliminate the possibility of external input and conclude that the culture developed on its own. The development of one-crop farming in the Diquis area and the Central Highlands provides an example of this logical process. Intensive maize agriculture caught on in Costa Rica about two thousand years after it began in Mesoamerica and Peru. Nevertheless, because Costa Rica's transition from diverse, small-plot farming on mountain slopes to almost exclusive maize cultivation in river valleys came gradually, not suddenly as it would have if caused by exposure to foreign ideas, archaeologists maintain that Costa Rican Indians developed single-crop farming independently. Though debate continues, archaeological circles now favor the opinion that internal mechanisms dominated in the development of Costa Rican Indian societies, even during times of great external influence.

🏛 🏛 🏛

40

III

Western Contact and Colonial Times

In the fall of 1502, toward the middle of his fourth, final voyage, Columbus threw anchor off the present site of Limón and, in what must count among history's worst misjudgments, described the land destined to become the poorest colony in New Spain as a place of superlative riches. Since 1492, Columbus had scudded around the Caribbean futilely looking for *the* mine, *the* river that provided all the natives' apparent wealth. Doubtless he had learned to say, "Where is the gold?" in a dozen dialects. Yet he had failed to learn that, while the natives inevitably thought they had a great deal of gold, indeed, their supplies could never fill the coffers of his imagination.

From Cariay to Costa Rica

The natives called the explorer's landfall Cariay, and as they testified to great ore deposits in the interior, Columbus tarried off its coast for eighteen days. His brother Bartholomew attempted to establish an outpost from which the Spaniards could explore the hinterland, but hostile tribes drove him back to the ships. Columbus's desire, it seems, compounded by Indians' promise of gold and their fierce repulsion of his scouting party, painted a picture of fantastic, well-defended booty. This picture endured in the minds of later explorers, who embellished the myth of the area's wealth by changing its name from Cariay to Costa Rica, the rich coast.

Despite Columbus's glowing reports, no Spaniard set foot in the region again for fourteen years; the death of the great patron Queen Isabel in 1504 temporarily shut down all exploration. Interest in the New World rose again, however, when King Ferdinand returned from his battles against the Italians. The king needed money, like all monarchs after a war; with an eye to the gold it might bring him, he set about planning the colonization of what the map makers called *Tierra Firme,* the Central American mainland.

In 1508, Ferdinand assigned a governor, Diego de Nicuesa, to explore the area from modern-day Honduras to modern-day Panama, including Cariay, lying in the middle. Optimistically, the explorers called the new province Castillo de Oro—Golden Castile. Partly due to starvation, disease, and Indian attack, but mainly due to treachery, incompetence, and greed, Nicuesa's expedition failed and he perished. To replace him, the Crown sent perhaps the most obtuse, cruel, and repulsive man ever to rule in the New World, Pedro Arias de Avila.

The atrocities Pedro Arias committed against the Indians and his shortsighted abuse of subordinates delayed the successful exploration and subjugation of both Panama, the colony's home base, and Costa Rica to the north. Arias de Avila opposed all capable adventurers, favoring instead those who made plunder their career and pillage their hobby. Among his gang of despoilers, only one, Gaspar de Espinosa, even imitated a discoverer. He sailed up the Pacific side of Costa Rica in 1516, making just enough contact with the natives and the shore to collect gold and provisions.

The first significant exploration of Costa Rica occurred in 1522, when Gil Gonzalez de Avila (no relation to Pedro Arias) marched from Panama to Nicaragua, exploring the entire Pacific coast of Costa Rica on the way. Gonzalez de Avila arrived at the provincial capital near the current location of the Panama Canal with a royal order commanding Pedro Arias de Avila to provide him with ships and other supplies. Hating nothing more than a man of obvious ability, the treacherous governor ignored the order and delayed the adventurer's departure for two years, finally delivering vessels so eaten by worms that, immediately upon setting sail, Gonzalez had to beach them for repairs just south of the present Costa Rican border. Making plans to rendezvous with his ships later, he took a hundred men and trudged inland.

All Spaniards—in fact, all Europeans—maltreated the Indians, and Gonzalez was no exception in this tradition. However, he did employ a modicum of diplomacy in his dealings with the natives, meaning that he tried to extort gold from them by peaceful means *before* kidnapping the chief or burning the village. By this method, Gonzales explored more territory with a hundred men in five months than Pedro Arias did with thousands of men in years.

When Gonzales and his party crossed the great Diquis River delta, rains fell so heavily that the leader succumbed to illness in the wet climate and had to be carried. While the men were crossing, the waters rose about them to form an island from a section of the delta, stranding the party for two weeks. As they traveled on, Gonzales encountered in the region what all subsequent explorers would: numerous petty chieftains with little gold and few subjects to convert.

After his foray into the country, Gonzales marched all the way to the Gulf of Nicoya, where he met his ships. Instead of sailing back to Panama, however, he chose to strike inland again, finding there the kind of Indian settlement that Spaniards could sink their teeth into. A chief named Nicoya, after whom Gonzales named the area and the gulf, ruled over six thousand subjects and possessed hundreds of gold trinkets. Wealth for the Crown paired prizes for the cross: the chief and his followers converted to Christianity (although their sincerity and understanding of the religion remain questionable) and gave the Spaniards as much gold as they had.

After a few weeks, Nicoya directed Gonzales northward to an even more powerful chief named Nicaragua, who had as much gold as the explorers could steal and good land with plentiful slaves to work it for them. Subsequent enterprises in this area would use the lands of Nicoya principally as a path to Nicaragua beyond. Ultimately, the descendants of Nicoya were trod over as well; the Spanish enslaved most of them to work in the Peruvian mines, and the rest perished by disease or in battle.

Thus far, conquistadors had tried only the Pacific approach to the country. Fittingly, it was Columbus's descendants, as if in an act of nostalgia, who sponsored the first exploration from the Atlantic coast. Since Columbus's death in 1506, his descendants had sued the crown in the Spanish courts for

legal rights to all the lands he discovered, rights that would have made his heirs more powerful than the monarchy itself. Needless to say, Columbus's family lost. But in 1534, as a minor concession, they won the right to rule, for twenty years, an area that the Crown legally separated from Nicaragua and officially named Costa Rica.

The heirs' appointed governor, Diego Gutierrez, led the most disastrous expedition in the conquest of Costa Rica. Ascending the Rio Suerre, he and his followers soon wore out their welcome with the natives. When Gutierrez pressured them, the tribes burned their own crops and took to the mountains, leaving some of the adventurers to starve and some to succumb to cannibalism. In a do-or-die effort, Gutierrez pressed on into the interior. The Indians waited until the group was too weak to resist and slaughtered all but seven of the Spaniards.

In 1562, the Crown handed the job of Costa Rica's permanent colonization to a man of true capacity and vision, Juan Vasquez de Coronado. Unlike any other European who had tried to explore and settle the area, Coronado had a plan—a plan so ingenious that it defined the Costa Rican landscape for all time. Instead of settling on the malarial coasts and from there striking into the interior, as his predecessors had, Coronado moved the principal settlement inland to the Meseta Central, founding Cartago in 1564. There, he established an agricultural community from which he could explore the rest of the country, funding it with his own money and, when that ran out, with heavy borrowing.

The Indians of the central valley submitted gradually to Coronado's occupation, partly because he did not too severely mistreat them, and partly because European diseases had decimated their populations and disturbed their social structures. The natives' cooperation, or at least their lack of serious resistance, allowed Coronado and his men to explore the entire Meseta Central and much of the surrounding territory. He gathered a lot of gold and in 1565 returned to Spain for financial backing. After hearing proof of the region's pacification, the Crown appointed Coronado governor-for-life. Unfortunately, the farsighted explorer's return ship sank at sea, and Spanish Costa Rica lost its greatest patron to date. With Coronado's passing, the conquest of Costa Rica practically ended. From that point forward, the colonists had more use for farmers than soldiers as they faced the difficult task of surviving in the poorest colony of New Spain.

THE POOREST COLONY IN NEW SPAIN

Although the Spanish eagerly sought Costa Rica as a conquest, they ignored and abused the place after surveying its lack of mineral wealth and Indian labor. The colony's poverty notwithstanding, they taxed and tithed, enforcing at the same time royal trade monopolies that made profitable commerce nearly impossible. Pirate raids further limited Spanish settlers' commercial opportunities; with undefended ports, the colonists found themselves completely cut off from

The Conquest That Skipped Costa Rica

❈

*T*he Costa Rican landscape hid no large ore deposits and supported only small, militantly territorial Indian populations, difficult to defeat in battle and impossible to enslave. These "shortcomings" ensured that Costa Rica never caught the first wave of the Spanish conquest, with its violence and decades-long struggle for power among the three main classes sent to conquer the New World: fighters, clerics, and government officials. 🏛 In 1565, long after the Spanish crown had abolished Indian enslavement and set other limits on the unofficially declared war against the Indians, Spain finally got a foothold in Costa Rica. Once settled, the conquistadors' inability to enslave Indians minimized friction with the church. The military left soon enough, anyway, looking for more profitable areas. Because of the sparse Indian population, the Catholic church never sent many representatives into the territory. As for the state, it merely administered the activities of farmers. Subsequently, the Costa Rican army, church, and colonial government never split into independent power blocks within the ranks of the ruling class. Elite power struggles erupted between rival families or regional factions, but not in the classic Latin American form of general vs. bishop vs. president.

🏛 🏛 🏛

48

Caribbean trade routes. To rule over this chaos, the Spanish Crown sent uninspired, untalented, old war veterans, who, in many instances, made the situation worse.

These harsh circumstances created great opportunity for the colonists as well as great hardship. The local aristocrats, almost as poor as their peasant subordinates, had to labor on their own land, producing in Costa Rican society a curious blend of elitism and egalitarianism. Abandoned by the Empire, colonial leaders became fiercely independent. The Indian population that proved too small to enslave was also too small to form an inconvenient minority. Natives who didn't die or move beyond the frontier assimilated into the mass, making the settlement racially and culturally homogeneous, an anomaly in a hemisphere torn by racial strife. These quirks of the colonial era—an aristocracy that was democratic by necessity, regional independence, and cultural cohesion—set Costa Rica apart from its neighbors, defining the character of the nation to come.

The People

From the 1560s, in an effort to expand their empire, Spanish conquistadors brought simple farmers and low-level gentry to settle Costa Rica's subjected territories. Since such impoverished domain attracted very few additional immigrants, these Spanish pioneers provided the population base for the entire colony. They attempted to settle in almost every region of the country at first, but by 1610 had established permanent towns in the Central Valley only. Indian hostility and unhealthy tropical weather had beaten the Spanish elsewhere, but in the milder climate and level geography of Costa Rica's center, they found an atmosphere suited to their temperaments and farming methods.

Once established, the Spanish settlers successfully imposed their culture upon Costa Rica within two generations. By 1600, no native Indian culture existed outside the Talamancas, the mountainous region in the southernmost part of the territory. To accomplish such absolute dominion, Spanish leaders throughout the New World invented a combination of apartheid and feudalism called the *encomienda* system. As a reward for services, or simply by purchase, *hidalgos* (nobles) received an *encomienda*, a section of land and certain demands on the Indians residing upon it. Indians were forced to donate labor and tribute to their Spanish *encomiendero*. And although natives on each land grant were segregated into settlements away from the Spanish landholders, they had to convert to Catholicism and adopt European ways.

But, despite such efforts, segregation was not absolute. Initial Spanish immigration had included many Spanish women, yet miscegenation proceeded at a rapid pace. European settlers came to the New World hoping to profit from, or at worst, exploit their black slaves and the native Indian population. In the end, they interbred with the objects of their economic desire. By the late colonial period these three separate races melded to form a homogeneous people—the Ticos.

From the outset, racial intermixing complicated an already confusing colonial social order. The Spanish Crown had created a new group of nobility to rule the New World, one by necessity less elite than the older aristocracy. Any meritorious person with maternal blood ties to a conquistador could claim noble rank. Unintentionally, this rule allowed the *hidalgo* class to maintain its integrity while accommodating miscegenous unions, bastard offspring, and social climbing by wealthy plebeians. Permeable class barriers in combination with shared racial origins provided great cohesion between *hidalgos* and *campesinos* (peasants) of Costa Rica, an exceptional partnership in the larger Central American experience.

Sources of Poverty

Running an empire takes a lot of money, and the Spanish conquistadors set out to make the American colonies pay their own way and, in addition, to earn a profit. Although some New World colonies with large Indian populations and valuable export commodities became self-sufficient and lucrative, Costa Rica failed on both fronts. Its settlers and Indians were so poor that their taxes, while a great burden to them, never covered the expenses of colonial administration. Unenthusiastic churchgoers, Costa Ricans tithed so illiberally that they left the local church destitute. Unsuccessful exporters and merchants, they donated meager tariff revenues to royal coffers.

The lack of a healthy export economy, caused in part by the Empire's restrictive economic policies, kept Costa Rica impoverished and out of touch. Spanish laws regulating colonial commerce existed before its first settlements. By writ, colonies could only trade with Spain, not with other European countries and only in a limited way with fellow colonies. Monopoly-holding Spanish merchants paid low prices for exports and charged high prices for imports, making official trade inherently unprofitable. Illicit trade with English, Dutch, and French traders brought more profits and cheaper goods, but the risks involved made it impractical on a large scale.

Despite these drawbacks, the sixteenth and seventeenth centuries saw trade develop in cattle, cocoa, subsistence goods, and mules. Trading activities were limited more by Costa Rica's virtually impassable land trails than by all the Empire's regulations put together. Residents of the Meseta Central communicated to ocean ports and to Nicaragua and Panama only by treacherous mountain trails, many of which washed out during the long rainy season. Such inconstant arteries of transport made the flow of commerce quite slow, but the money-hungry Spanish government nevertheless refused to fund the building of better trails.

Ironically, Costa Rican settlers saw bad trails as a benefit, since their ill repair helped defend the colony against pirate and Indian raids that disrupted the region from the seventeenth century until its independence. After taking over Jamaica in 1655, British warships began preying on Spanish shipping lanes and plundering vulnerable port towns.

𝒩ature, no doubt, hates nothing more than a wall; Spanish immigrants, it seems, hated nothing more than nature, so they raised walls to keep it out. Mortar and stone physically blocked the jungle, but the Spanish settlers built cities as moral fortification against the anarchy of pagan wilderness. While Costa Rican colonists had too little money and too few people to fund or justify a bona fide city, they nevertheless expressed the obsessive Spanish preference for centralized settlement. 🏛 The abundant water and good soil of the Meseta Central would have prompted a governor in the mold of Thomas Jefferson to divide the area into even plots and give a homestead to every farmer in the colony. The Spanish authorities, civil and ecclesiastical, did the opposite, discouraging dispersed settlement as much as they could. The bishop threatened to excommunicate all outlying farmers who would not form or join nucleated communities. Those unimpressed by the promise of perdition had their dwellings burnt to the ground. 🏛 By these extreme measures, colonial government strove to recreate on foreign soil the world it had known in Spain. Cartago, the colony's

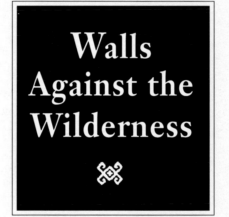

Walls Against the Wilderness

principal town, even duplicated the structure of a Castilian farming hamlet. The elite privately held land surrounding the town, while the peons paid rent to use common planting and pasture grounds. Although ample farmland lay just beyond the elite holdings, social and legal pressures forced the Spanish peasants to accept near landlessness and poverty within town boundaries rather than move out and farm a plot of their own. 🏛 The perpetuation of this archaic system of land tenure did not merely satisfy the colonists' nostalgia for rural Castile. It also upheld a social hierarchy made almost invisible by the poverty of all the colonists from governor to peon, and it generated a landless (or, at least, land-poor) peasantry whose labor could be used by the elite. The colony's urban concentration also allowed the church to enforce adherence to ritual and allowed the state to tax more efficiently. Despite its disadvantages for many, the Costa Ricans valued the social clarity of village life too much to leave it, at least until coffee came along and changed the value of everything.

🏛 🏛 🏛

53

54

Instead of rebuilding and fortifying Costa Rican ports, the Spanish authorities of the 1660s abandoned the Caribbean coast, forcing most settlers in the coastal hinterlands to evacuate and all but shutting down lowland cocoa production. Such precautions completely isolated Costa Rica from the rest of the Empire and, unfortunately, did not deter all raiders.

In 1666, the French pirate Mansvelt and his second in command, the now-famous Henry Morgan, landed on the Atlantic coast with the unlikely plan to march inland and sack Cartago. They had set out from Jamaica to take the Panamanian town, Natá, but that port's defenses repulsed them. A Spaniard whom they had captured and used as a guide proposed to lead them to Cartago, ensuring them it had wealth and few armaments. So they struck the Caribbean coast around modern-day Limón and turned inland. The march went well until the pirates reached the mountains, where, starving and quarreling, they encountered a tiny force of Costa Rican defenders who had staked out the ridge above Turrialba.

The Costa Ricans attacked in the morning, probably a bad time of day for pirates, and scattered the whole bunch with one volley of fire. Pursuing those who fled, the Costa Ricans captured some stragglers, who upon interrogation divulged that they had run, at least in part, because a giant, radiant form of the Virgin Mary had floated above the Costa Rican forces during the attack. Though the pirates only recollected this miracle under torture, the colonists took it as a propitious sign. For decades, Spanish settlers made pilgrimages to the church of the bellicose Virgin of Ujarras.

Pirates never again got that close to the Costa Rican heartland, but Indians continued to harass Caribbean settlements throughout the nineteenth century. The Miskito Indians of the Nicaraguan lowlands had begun to attack Costa Rican Caribbean communities and plantations as soon as they formed. With British backing in the late seventeenth and early eighteenth centuries, their raids became more frequent and more destructive. By 1779 these attacks had so effectively disrupted cocoa production and cut off the Meseta from the coast that the governor of Costa Rica agreed to pay tribute to the Miskito king to stop them, a payment that continued until 1841.

The Leadership

Paying off the marauding Miskitos signified less a surrender to violence and more the belated recognition that Costa Rica, while not rich in gold, was worth something. The earliest governors, principally explorers, measured a land only in pesos of gold, so they had no use for the misnamed Costa Rica. To replace these disenchanted conquistadors, the Spanish government sent generals who had retired from European campaigns and who apparently did not have enough clout in the royal palace to get better appointments. Old war horses out to pasture made bad colonial administrators to begin with, and most cared too little to try to do better. At best, they collected taxes. Occasionally, with money that

could have improved trails or started much needed economic ventures, one of them oiled up his sword and tried to pacify the Indians in the Talamancan Mountains, a mission that inevitably failed.

By 1709, administrative indifference, lack of mercantile opportunity, and an empire-wide depression had driven the Costa Rican economy so far down that residents began to use cocoa beans as currency, as Nicoyan Indians had done at the time of European contact. At this lowest moment in the colony's history, events in Spain actually assisted its recovery. The Hapsburg line, which had ruled Spain since the death of King Ferdinand in 1516, died out, in part because of inbreeding. The offshoot of the Bourbon line that inherited the Spanish throne came from mainstream Europe and imported many free-thinking, liberal ideas then in vogue. Although these ideas took decades to affect colonial administration, the spirit of the anticipated reforms infected the colonial leadership much earlier.

Unlike many of his predecessors, Diego de la Haya Fernández, who governed Costa Rica from 1718 to 1727, did care about the colony. He also had enough talent to produce changes. Reopening the ports and defending regions of cocoa production against attack, he even got roads and bridges repaired. His successors followed his example, and the coming reforms from Spain justified their improvements. Early in the eighteenth century, the Bourbons lifted limits on commerce among the colonies; later, they opened American trade to all Spanish ports.

55

Increased trade revenues improved the general condition of the colony, made a few people rich (mostly Spanish immigrants), and gave a little more power to the local elite. Through intermarriage and social intercourse, the Tico aristocracy had always maintained bonds with the sources of political power—Spanish government officials and foreign merchants—but as a distinct group the elite had had little influence. The new prosperity increased the importance of the municipal councils they controlled, and although this did not immediately give the aristocracy any more political clout, these empowered councils would play a crucial role in Costa Rica's transition from colony to nation.

Liberals vs. Conservatives

In the eighteenth and nineteenth centuries the terms "liberal" and "conservative" mainly referred to opinions about how a country should run its economy. Conservatives wanted the state, the church, and the military to control all land, wealth, and commerce, as these institutions had for centuries. Aristocrats could partake of riches and power by joining these centers of power. Liberals, on the other hand, wished to divest these institutions of their exclusive control and create a free market. In a liberal economy, wealth and power shifted away from conservative institutions toward foreign investors and the domestic elite, the only groups with enough resources to take advantage of a free market.

Spanish colonial officials—therefore conservative power—resided in Cartago. From there, the officials handed out appointments, trade monopolies, the rights to collect taxes and tithes, and other royal advantages to preferred members of the local aristocracy. Available privileges were limited, especially in a colony as poor as Costa Rica, so some of the elite engaged in contraband trade, mostly selling tobacco and cocoa beans to the British. In 1755, incensed colonial officials banished the *contrabandistas* twenty miles west of Cartago, over the Ochomogo Height. This act marked the end of Cartago's dominance, since the spirit of modern Costa Rica followed the smugglers and settled with them in their new town—San José.

The main difference between Cartago and San José, apart from the occupants, lay in the organization of the land. Cartago resembled a feudal village: peasants rented common lands, and the elite held privately all the surrounding property. Around San José, the land remained for the most part unstructured, unclaimed, uncultivated. So San José could easily change from a subsistence farming village to a community of market-oriented agricultural producers (of tobacco predominantly); Cartago could not.

Fortune smiled on the smugglers when in 1766 Crown authorities granted Costa Rica the tobacco monopoly for the northern Central American region. A few years later, the Spanish built a tobacco plant in San José, giving the newly chartered city official commercial status. But San José did not need this official sanction; Costa Rican conservative institutions were not strong enough to stand against the wind of liberal change.

Independence

Costa Ricans did not participate in their independence from Spain; they were informed of it. On October 13, 1821, a letter arrived by mule from Guatemala, stating that Costa Rica had no more ties to Spain. In other colonies, the question of independence had prompted bloody power struggles between conservative imperialists who benefited from Spanish rule and liberal Republicans who wanted to join the world of nations. Costa Ricans, though divided into the same camps, had not been asked the question of independence. Their freedom was unanticipated, so they had nothing to fight about . . . yet.

Eventually the Costa Ricans did struggle, not over independence, but over joining the Mexican Empire, when Mexican military leader Augustín de Iturbide sought to unite Mexico and Central America under one flag. Costa Rican conservatives saw membership in this empire as a chance to preserve the structure of the old colonial government. Liberals saw a move from Spanish rule to Mexican rule as jumping from the frying pan into the fire. At least Spain lay across an ocean; the distance allowed liberals certain illicit freedoms. The promoters of a free market believed Iturbide's empire would likely reverse gains made since the 1760s.

Fearing invasion, the liberals tolerated Costa Rican submission to Iturbide for two years. Then, in March 1823, they led the collected town councils in declaring independence. Infuriated Cartagan imperialists revolted, taking over the

government in Cartago and commandeering the government armory. Thus prepared, they marched toward San José, where a similar force had mustered in response. The two sides met on the Ochomogo Height. Three and a half hours and twenty-one dead later, the San José liberals stood triumphant—Costa Rica no longer belonged to the Mexican Empire, and Costa Rica's capital was moved to San José. Ironically, Iturbide had abdicated three weeks before this decisive battle, the slow mail once more leaving Costa Ricans in the dark.

The dissolution of the short-lived empire did not quash the efforts of the former colonies to achieve political unity. In 1823, Costa Rica joined the Central American Federation—a liberal-dominated (therefore decentralized) political alliance headed by Guatemala. Costa Rican conservatives opposed membership in the federation from the start, and even liberals came to dislike having strong political ties to areas with different social problems and economic aspirations.

The federation had some advantages though. For one, Costa Ricans elected their own leader and in effect ruled themselves, so the federation allowed practice at nationhood, easing the transition from dependency to sovereignty. The union also gave the former colonies an opportunity to redefine their borders. In 1824, Guanacaste province voted to secede from Nicaragua and associate itself with Costa Rica. Such a reorganization might have prompted a war

between nations, but between federated states it transpired with a minimum of friction.

In 1934, the town councils of Heredia, Alajuela, and Cartago, resenting San José's dominance, forced a compromise over the location of the capital. Under the so-called Ambulatory Law, the capital would move from town to town every four years. Before the first move could be made, however, President Braulio Carrillo declared San José the permanent capital, disregarding the law. The other cities formed a league and attacked the city, but Carrillo's forces fought them off, ending forever all debate over the seat of national government.

Carrillo pulled Costa Rica from the Central American Federation in 1938, and the "rich coast" became a sovereign nation. A few months later, interregional violence caused the entire federation to collapse, marking the death of liberalism everywhere else in Central America. In Costa Rica, in the personality of Braulio Carrillo, it survived.

Seventeen years had elapsed in the transition from colony to nation. During that time, Costa Rica gained a province, Guanacaste. Costa Ricans discovered themselves unrelated to their fellow Central Americans, and until the modern era, shunned participation in pan-Central American affairs. The liberals of San José firmly established their predominance over other regional power groups. Finally, in these years the country took its first steps out of the economic backwater with the help of an imported African bean—coffee.

58

IV

Coffee! Costa Rica's First Revolution

From its independence in 1821 to the modern era, Costa Rica has seen its growth pulled by the engine of coffee. As a colony, Costa Rica lay suspended in a nascent state, with no characteristic industry, no wealth, no all-powerful ruling class. But soon after independence, its Ticos discovered gold and silver in the Aguacate Mountains. More importantly, they found the golden bean—coffee. The Ticos' reactions to newfound wealth created by export of this roasted plant seed made Costa Rica's early statehood a period of profound development, an era from which the country derived many of its exceptional qualities.

Without an established market, coffee built its consumer base slowly. Exports in the 1920s to Panama and in the 1930s to Chile did not create a boom, but did pique the interest of foresighted business and government leaders. San José colonial official Maríano Montealegre, who oversaw tobacco production for the Spanish Empire, supervised the planting of tens of thousands of coffee trees, against the advice of many Ticos who regarded his enthusiasm as folly. Astutely anticipating future demand, Montealegre and other San José businessmen, like Juan Rafael Mora Porras, became Costa Rica's top producers when the markets opened up. Politicians also fostered the fledgling industry. When Braulio Carrillo, national leader from 1835 to 1842, began distributing municipal lands around San José to aspiring small landholders, he made the planting of coffee a prerequisite for acquiring free plots. Leaders like Carrillo saw coffee as Costa Rica's best hope for economic advance, so they imbued coffee cultivation with patriotic overtones.

Despite these various encouragements, the coffee industry still did not boom, mainly because trade with Chile brought low profits. Chilean merchants bought beans at a low price from Costa Rican growers, then processed and sold them to Europe as Chilean coffee. By 1929 coffee had become Costa Rica's major export, but the dissatisfactory arrangement with Chile discouraged farmers, delaying the full development of the coffee industry until Tico exporters established their own connections to European markets.

That connection was made accidentally. In 1843, the British ship *Monarch*, bound for Liverpool, docked in Puntarenas harbor. The boat was loaded with pelts from Canada, but needed ballast to make it around South America's stormy tip. Its captain trekked to San José, where growers gave him 500,000 pounds of coffee on credit. Landing in Liverpool, the captain sold his coffee ballast quickly; a few months later, when he returned to Costa Rica, the enterprising Ticos earned huge profits on their risk. This windfall shipment inspired the coffee boom. Within a generation, Costa Ricans changed centuries-old patterns of land use and social practice to facilitate coffee production. Halfway around the world, British investors moved quickly to support the shipping end of the business.

LAND CRAZY AND LABOR SHY

Costa Rica was ready for coffee. Because nineteenth-century Costa Rica lacked a wealth-generating industry to compete with the golden bean, no special interests fought against coffee expansion. Furthermore, none of the country's elite had made fortunes in the conservative colonial era, so even the most conservative among them favored liberal economic policies that fostered capitalistic growth. Business and government leaders faced one grave obstacle to increased coffee cultivation: almost eighty percent of the Meseta Central remained covered by forest. With no ready work force able to clear the land, the coffee capitalists reached for another solution. Over time, they transformed the country's land-poor peasants into an army of small-time agrarian capitalists, drastically altering Costa Rican society.

Lacking the landless masses that toiled for pennies in northern Central American nations, the Costa Rican elite constantly lamented their inability to secure ready workers. Without single laborers, the emerging capitalist order had to enlist families as working units. Costa Rican homestead laws gave families more than one thousand acres of land each, with a catch—settlers gained title to their plots only after converting the wilderness into a farm. Carrillo and Costa Rican leaders after him also ensured that peasants who took advantage of the laws planted coffee. Thus the land came under cultivation, with coffee springing up across the Meseta Central.

The central valley filled quickly with farms, when, from the 1830s to the 1890s, upwardly mobile peasants emptied out of the old central settlements to try their luck on the frontier. Within a generation, Costa Rica changed from an essentially urban-based society to a dispersed rural society, with migrants mainly populating excellent coffee lands around Alajuela and westward. Because Ticos divided their homesteads equally among their children, second generation migrants faced the same choice as their parents: stay put and subsist, or expand along the frontier.

This peasant diaspora exacerbated the labor shortage in older areas, thereby binding the aristocracy and the peasants in a symbiotic relationship quite different to the paternalism of the colonial era. To secure the labor of surrounding small landholders, estate owners struck up personal relationships with their poorer neighbors and paid high wages. Likewise, coffee processors extended credit to peasant farmers because they needed the output from small farms to make their expensive processing plants profitable. For their part, small-landholding peasants could not have survived without income from the haciendas or financial help from processors. A typical peasant farmer could not raise enough food and cash crops to feed his family and pay for other needs. But small farms did not require all of a family's labor, so small landholders supplemented incomes by working on neighboring estates. By doing so, every member of a family, even children, could earn wages. Combining home production with seasonal labor, many Costa Rican peasants were relatively prosperous.

While Tico peasants turned the wilderness into coffee fields and themselves into a rural middle class, the elite

64

consolidated their control over the country. Before coffee, merchants and government officials held the highest places in Costa Rican society. Every aristocrat owned land as a badge of his or her class, but since landowning was unprofitable, the privileged classes never put much stock in it. This partly explains why wealthier nationals contentedly permitted peasants to gobble up much of the best coffee land. To the elite, even after coffee, real money did not come from the land. As coffee eclipsed the nation's other enterprises, aristocrats retained an affinity for mercantile and governmental positions, from which they could easily spread out into coffee processing, financing, and, of course, landowning. The wide power base of the coffee elite allowed them to quickly convert Costa Rica from a backward, colonial outpost to an efficient agro-exporting machine.

The linchpin of this machine was coffee processing. No factor— not soil, nor rainfall, nor altitude—affects the quality of an individual bean as much as processing. Processing plants, called *beneficios*, convert the ripe fruit into exportable green coffee beans using one of two methods. In the dry method, regarded as inferior, freshly picked beans bake in the sun for a few weeks, then are run through mills that remove the outer layers from the coffee. In wet-method *beneficios*, which produce a more consistent, superior grade of bean, husks and pulp are milled off before drying. The processors then ferment the membrane-covered seeds in water for thirty-six hours, removing the mucous layer afterward. They dry the beans only after fermenting to make green coffee.

Historically, wet-method and dry-method processing differed most in their operating costs. Anyone with a hand-mill or even a mortar and pestle could perform dry-method processing. The wet method, however, required a large factory with fermenting tanks and sluices that brought water in and out. The many steps in the wet process also demanded more labor. All of these factors made the wet method impossible without large capital investment. Yet, almost from the beginning, Costa Rican exporters only accepted beans processed by the wet method, because these commanded higher prices on the world market than dry-method beans.

Choosy exporters fetched more money for the farmers, but they also placed a handful of unified processors in a powerful position over Tico producers. Furthermore, processors were usually exporters as well, so they controlled two aspects of the national harvest. The elite of the elite, Costa Rica's *cafetaleros* (coffee barons) bought and sold overseas every bag of picked coffee and every processed bean; every farthing and pfennig that came into the country flowed through their hands. When farmers needed credit on their next crop, they borrowed from the *cafetalero* that ran the nearest *beneficio*. During harvests, small producers labored on the lands of *cafetaleros* to whom they owed money, injecting an element of coercion into the relationship between the two. Although the *cafetaleros'* absolute control deprived peasant farmers of equal social benefits, all participants in the coffee industry profited so generously during the era of land expansion that the underclass barely perceived the inequity.

Coffee Perfume

There are fifty different natural species of coffee, an evergreen shrub from northeast Africa and the adjacent Mideast. Of these species, only *Coffea arabica* has economic importance in Costa Rica. *Coffea arabica* grows at altitudes from two thousand to six thousand feet above sea level, requires an average temperature of 70° F, annual rainfall from forty to seventy inches, and a dry season of two to three months. Coffee trees break into fragrant, white flowers at the first rain after the dry season, usually in March. About eight months later, the fruit, technically a drupe or stonefruit like a cherry, ripens from green to red. Its red casing peels off to reveal a layer of pulp, which surrounds two small skin-covered seeds, the coffee beans. Once removed from these outer layers, the seeds dry in the sun to become green coffee, ready for roasting.

 Arguably the world's finest mild coffee, the large, high-acidity Costa Rican beans brew a full-bodied cup, substantial on the back of the tongue. Producers export mainly to the picky European market, which demands large, hand-sorted beans as opposed to the American market, which accepts both large and small machine-sorted beans. European coffee houses frequently use Costa Rican beans in blending because they provide a generous base for flavorful, idiosyncratic coffees like Tanzanian or Kenyan. Unlike the mild Columbian coffee that dominates the American market, Costa Rican coffee has a definite, perfumy aroma.

68

To grease the wheels of the coffee business, the Costa Rican upper class set up a liberal state that maintained a laissez-faire capitalist economy. Unlike their richer cousins in northern Central America who did not stoop to politics, *cafetaleros* also ran the government. The heads of the two most powerful coffee families, the Moras and the Montealegres, became presidents of the republic in the years between 1820 and the 1870s. But political offices were only the top of the coffee pyramid. Tico liberals honed every element of society to serve the coffee industry and sought to ruin those, such as the church, that didn't. They monopolized credit by fighting the establishment of a national bank; they preserved profits by keeping taxes low. Encouraging free trade (not imposing protective tariffs) to the detriment of local manufacturers, they effectively arrested any economic growth besides agro-export. To their credit, the elite diverted sizeable amounts of money into education and the country's infrastructure (roads and communication), but as a whole sought to benefit themselves, not common Ticos.

COFFEE POLITICS

Costa Rican politics had nothing to do with parties and everything to do with personality. In their relatively homogeneous country, members of the power elite often shared the same ideology as those out of power, so idea-based parties had little function. On the other hand, an individual with enough support could become elected and lead the government on the planks of charisma and class. Ultimately, though, a personality's constituency broke up into competing coalitions too narrow to support that individual's grip on the government, and the next leader stepped in. In this way, Costa Rican leaders starting with Braulio Carrillo gained and lost personal control of the country.

The two architects of the coffee state, Braulio Carrillo and Juan Rafael Mora Porras, ruled from 1835 to 1859. President Carrillo did the country a great favor by making San José the permanent capital, but the elite in outlying areas hated him for it. His enemies could not topple him, however, until he lost popularity by declaring himself dictator-for-life in 1841. After that announcement, his opponents obtained enough political backing to invite a Honduran military hero to enter Costa Rica and depose him. The general that Carrillo sent to quash the invasion joined the interloper instead, helping oust his old boss.

Coup begets coup, and the nation languished in chaos until 1847, when twenty-nine-year-old José María Castro Madriz became president. A vigorous reformer, Castro championed the education system and turned the army into a national guard. His reforms angered the *cafetaleros*, and his emasculation of the military angered the generals, so the two factions joined to end his presidency. In 1849, one of the coup leaders and a top-ranking *cafetalero*, Juan Rafael Mora Porras, ascended to the presidency. For a decade Mora provided a stable, nurturing environment for the Costa Rican coffee business.

President Mora made his most important contribution to Costa Rican history in 1856 by initiating a military adventure that galvanized the country's divisive regional interests into a unified national consciousness. When disgruntled Tennessee slave owner William Walker and his North American mercenaries invaded Nicaragua in an attempt to increase the number of U.S. slave states, threatening the Costa Rican border, Mora dispatched an army of nine thousand men. Taking the offensive, the Ticos crossed the northern border into Nicaragua, cutting off Walker's invaders, who were headed for Guanacaste. At Rivas, Nicaragua, the North Americans abandoned their position after Juan Santamaría, a boy from a poor Alajuelan peasant family, set their headquarters on fire. Dying in the attempt, Santamaría became a national hero, but he had not ended the war. When the mercenaries returned to Rivas a few months later, Costa Rican forces had to join with Nicaraguan armies to drive them out of the area for good.

Ironically, this enormously popular war sped the demise of President Mora. After the war ended, the surviving troops returned triumphant to San José laden with battle stories and cholera. Ten percent of Costa Rica's population died in the ensuing plague, and the tales of the soldiers told why. Mismanagement and corruption on the part of campaign leaders had turned a routine excursion into a wretched disaster—more men had died in the squalid camps than in the fighting. The fallout from this scandal and from the epidemic landed directly on Mora's head. Exacerbating the anger of the Costa Rican people, he had recently alienated a group of elite by proposing to charter a national bank, which would have undercut the *cafetaleros'* credit monopoly. Taking advantage of his unpopularity, his enemies unseated the president in a military coup, placing the head of the rival Montealegre family in office.

President José María Montealegre Fernández (1859-1863) and his successors continued on the path marked by Mora, further tailoring the Costa Rican economy to serve narrow coffee interests. But unlike Mora, Montealegre had to deal with an increasingly interfering army clique. The war and the following coup gave the military more power than it had ever had or would ever have again. The battles had created several heros who intended to capitalize on their elevated status. For the first time in Costa Rican history, the military became a partner in power with the upper class.

Throughout the 1860s, President Montealegre and a succession of puppet presidents tried unsuccessfully to pull in the reins of the army. Finally, in 1870, the populist General Tomás Guardia Gutierrez took the government in a coup. Instead of setting another *cafetalero* in the top spot, however, he took the presidential position himself. He ruled from 1870-1882, declaring himself "dictator-for-life" after the first four years because a cherished Costa Rican tradition forbade "presidents" to hold office for consecutive terms.

Enemy to the self-interested *cafetaleros*, President Guardia planned from the outset not merely to usurp their role for a time but to end their rule altogether. To curb governmental

influence of the coffee barons, he abolished many political freedoms, reversing the national trend toward democratization at the polls. To weaken their economic stranglehold on the country, Guardia broadened the trade beyond coffee and even dabbled in redistributing land from large holdings back to peasant farmers. To prevent any more military takeovers, he disempowered the army.

President Guardia's most lasting contribution to Costa Rica, however, resulted from his indefatigable quest for a railway from the Meseta to the Atlantic—the Jungle Train. Until the 1880s, coffee had been transported down a cart road to Puntarenas, then onto ships, around the Horn, and finally to Europe. Guardia's railway to the Atlantic increased export volume and provided a direct link to the European market. Finished after his death, the railroad also had its side effects—a multi-million dollar national debt (Costa Rica's first), a foreign-owned lowland banana industry, and a permanent population of Jamaican expatriate laborers.

President Guardia's successors continued his spirit of reform. President Próspero Fernández Oreamuno (1882-1885), Guardia's brother-in-law, wiped out church power by taking away church property, secularizing schools, and legislating a complete separation between church and state. President Fernández's death did not halt the reform. Intent on educating all Costa Ricans, not just sons of the elite, President Bernardo Soto Alfaro (1885-1889) made Costa Rica the first country in Central America to establish mandatory, free, primary and secondary education. Ironically, because of

monetary considerations, President Soto closed down the San Tomás University at the same time, reasoning that the country did not need a college if most of its people could not read.

Although President Guardia and his followers ruled as autocrats, not democrats, they managed through vigorous reforms to make Costa Rica a more democratic nation. In 1889, President Soto, who honored the cherished Tico political tradition of not running for a consecutive term, presided over an honestly counted, democratic election with an unfettered press and open discussion of issues. Handing the reigns of government to his rival, he provided the first peaceful transition of power in Costa Rican history.

CLOSING THE COFFEE FRONTIER

Costa Rica had made an astoundingly smooth transition from a village-based peasant society to a dispersed agrarian capitalist society—smooth because it involved no conflict between landless peons and great estate owners. So long as good coffee land remained available and coffee prices stayed high, the peasant masses remained upwardly mobile and had no need to butt heads with their "betters." Social differences gained rough edges as the land ran out around the turn of the century, illuminating conflicts between elite and peasant.

The land shortage curtailed coffee expansion, exacerbating problems with production and further confusing Costa Rican patterns of land ownership. Tico farmers did not grow

74

coffee with factory-like efficiency. To increase output, neither large nor small planters attempted to improve underproductive methods but instead simply acquired more land. Adjacent land rarely came up for purchase, so as farmers added on they fragmented their holdings into several separate plots. This made the farms even harder to work efficiently. Most significantly, land scarcity froze geographical expansion. Young Ticos at the turn of the century had no choice but to leave their subdivided holdings and migrate to areas offering only subsistence farming and wage labor.

This sharp downturn in the fortunes of once-prosperous coffee peasants coincided disastrously with a worldwide coffee slump from the 1890s to the 1920s. When prices dropped, processors maintained profit margins by passing their losses to the small farmers. The resiliency of small producers, which came from their ability to over- or under-exploit family labor made Costa Rica almost recession-proof in the early twentieth century. Ultimately, however, the peasants acted against the abuses of the *cafetaleros*, not through riots and revolution, but through the political process. Following President Guardia, the reigning liberal politicians gave peasants a stake in Tico democracy, convincing most that revolution was not a worthwhile alternative.

THE GENERATION OF '89

President Guardia undoubtedly reformed Costa Rica.

More importantly, his time in power tutored the aristocracy on the dangers of relying on a narrow power base. Chastened by the dictator's excesses, the second-generation coffee elite assumed control of the country with more respect for democracy. Educated in Europe, the sons and grandsons of the original planters returned home full of liberal inspiration. The self-named "Olimpio (Olympic) Generation" or "Generation of '89" (after the first year of their power) systematically improved education and broadened participation in the political process by liberalizing both press and polls. They undertook these reforms out of deep ideological conviction, but just as surely aimed to generate a wide-based political constituency that would stabilize the Costa Rican government and defend against another Guardia-like dictatorship.

From 1889 forward, the elite behaved according to the rules of a constitutional republic, not the rules of brute force. In order to maintain dominance as a group within the new Costa Rican politics, warring factions within the elite had to cooperate or compete openly. Rising literacy rates increased peasant demands for voting rights, and open competition further encouraged the lower class's appetite for political involvement by airing national debates in a public forum.

In 1892, Rafael Yglesias Castro, the first great leader of the new liberal aristocracy, ran against Costa Rica's first political party, the Catholic Union Party (PUC). Originally created to protect the church against the ravages of liberal anticlericalism, the PUC's ultimate platform hit on social injustice caused by economic liberalism. To counter the appeal of the PUC, Yglesias created his own Republican Party. Not characterized by a continuous ideological vision, the Republican Party merely acted as the instrument of the ruling elite faction. Despite its facade, the fact that the aristocracy ran beneath a party banner represented a serious compromise. Assisted by fraudulent vote-counting, Yglesias defeated the PUC candidate. But, without a real mandate, he could not rule as absolutely as his predecessors.

Though the elite fought against Guardia's policies for decades, once back in power they persisted after his example. President Yglesias's regime not only expanded education but went beyond Guardia by conceding political rights to peasants. The Generation of '89 also proceeded with expensive public-works projects. To complement the Jungle Train, they constructed rails connecting the Meseta Central with the Pacific port of Puntarenas. They spent well over a million dollars to equip Limón with a sewer system and to install public electric lighting in San José, which became the third city in the entire world to posess that amenity. Most extravagantly, as a paean perhaps to their restored power, the Olimpio Generation's coffee elite constructed the National Theater. The new generation even continued to favor foreign investors, particularly North Americans in the Atlantic banana enclaves. Unlike the Guardia regime, however, President Yglesias and his successors increasingly

debated these policy issues in public, taking popular opinion into account.

Costa Rica's trend towards a more open political process brought Ricardo Jiménez Oreamuno to power in 1910. A politically savvy populist, President Jiménez moved quickly to expand peasant participation while protecting the interests of his own class, the coffee elite. Decentralizing the government by giving outlying municipal authorities more control over their own affairs, Jiménez amended the constitution in 1913 to allow direct presidential elections. Thus encouraged, well-off peasants began to take active roles in local and then national politics.

When no clear winner emerged from Costa Rica's first direct presidential election in 1914, the Congress, in a typical Tico compromise, appointed a non-candidate to the presidency. Alfredo Flores initiated socially progressive policies that made him popular with common Ticos but rapidly eroded his support with the upper class. The final blow to President Flores came with World War I and the Allied blockade of Germany, which sent Costa Rican coffee prices tumbling. When Flores tried to place the financial burden of the ensuing depression on the wealthy, they rebelled against his authority and deposed him in a military coup. The elite's regression to raw power galvanized opposition from lower- and middle-class Tico reformers, setting the classes on a collision course that ended in the Revolution of 1948.

In everything he did, General Tomás Guardia aimed Costa Rica into the modern world. To change his country's political system from outdated paternalistic rule to genuine democracy, he broke the backs of the *cafetaleros*. President Guardia (1870-1882) centered this determined modernization of the Costa Rican economy around a railway from the Meseta Central to the Atlantic coast.
🏛 From independence, Costa Rican leaders worked to improve the country's roads. Guardia hoped to do this, too, but his vision went beyond cart tracks to a state-of-the-art railroad integrating Costa Rica and the international trade community. To get the best rail system, in 1871 Guardia sent his minister of public works to see Henry Meiggs, the American who built in the Peruvian Andes what remains the world's highest altitude railway. The Costa Rican minister never met Meiggs himself, however, dealing instead with his nephew, Henry Meiggs Keith. Despite the elder Meiggs's absence, negotiations proceeded smoothly. The minister soon returned with a contract that would, in three years, give Costa Rica a railroad from Alajuela to Limón for £1.6 million, its parts bought in Britain. 🏛 The Meiggs operation made railways, but it made money even better. Although wording of the agreement suggested that the famous Meiggs would do the work himself, the contractors intended from the beginning that his inexperienced nephew build the railroad alone. When construction

The Jungle Train

began in 1871, President Guardia accepted this change of personnel, perhaps influenced by the fact that he had received £100,000 in kickbacks for signing the contract. With a small bribe, the Meiggs operation bamboozled the Costa Ricans into paying for the original Meiggs but getting his more youthful imitation. Not surprisingly, Henry Meiggs Keith failed to build the railroad. Worthless and indolent as well as inexperienced, he quit Costa Rica in 1873, having constructed only the tracks from Alajuela to Cartago—a section of road across flat terrain that a Costa Rican engineer could have managed. 🏛 By the time Henry Keith's failure came to light, the Ticos had a larger problem than their lack of railroad: a crippling national debt. To pay Meiggs, Guardia had sent his finance minister to borrow from the hostile jungle of European finance. The minister got mauled and European financiers got rich. The Costa Rican government received about £1 million, not nearly enough to pay for the £1.6 million railroad, at usurious rates of interest that drove the actual debt from this loan up to £4 million. This large encumbrance made lenders unwilling to make further loans, leaving Guardia to finance further building on his own. Fortunately, Henry Keith left behind the equipment needed to finish the rails; more importantly, he left behind his brother—a man who would make his fortune and a railroad in Costa Rica. 🏛 Minor Keith, younger nephew of Henry

Meiggs, had a spark in him that his brother lacked. Running the workers' commissary in Limón during his brother's abortive attempt to build the trans-national railroad, he succeeded in several lucrative side ventures. By the time Henry Keith departed, Minor Keith was a businessman in his own right who could have added to his earnings the leftover operating funds of the then-defunct commissary. He might have taken this small fortune of over $200,000 American and quit Costa Rica after his brother, but various opportunities kept him in the country. 🏛 Minor Keith's persistence expedited development of two sympathetic ventures that would make his fortune and get Guardia his coffee conduit to the Atlantic—bananas and rail construction. In the early 1870s, Keith cultivated bananas in the Limón region. This proved so profitable that when President Guardia contracted an American engineering firm in 1875 to complete a leg of the railroad, Keith bankrolled the construction. Ultimately the original company gave up the project, so, to save his investment, the inexperienced Keith finished the work himself. Success in the project made him the General's man. Guardia gave Keith every subsequent construction job, and the American extended the line some forty miles into the highlands. When government money ran out, Keith built a highway to Cartago connecting the two sections of railroad. 🏛 Minor Keith got other public-works contracts as well, building the Limón sewer system and installing tramways and electric lighting in San José. As Keith extended the railroad farther from Limón with government contracts, he expanded his banana business alongside the tracks. In turn, his extremely lucrative banana trade incited him to take more government contracts, which by themselves did not turn a fantastic profit. 🏛 Both construction and banana cultivation required abundant labor. Ticos spoiled by the cool highlands would not descend into the humid, tropical lowlands to work, so Keith had to rely on laborers from abroad, principally Jamaican blacks. In the late 1800s, former slaves from British colony islands began to spread outward from their Caribbean homelands to the greater Americas. Black expatriates became the vagabonds of the age, settling temporarily where the work paid best—plantation enclaves, construction projects. Unhappily for Keith, the unsuccessful French attempt from 1878 to 1888 to dig a canal through the isthmus of Panama offered much higher wages than he did. Costa Rican construction projects could not match French ones, partly from lack of funds but primarily from fear of inflating the wages of the country's coffee workers who no doubt would have demanded increases. 🏛 With the available labor force passing up Costa Rica for Panama, Minor Keith spent hundreds of thousands of U.S. dollars transporting laborers to Limón. Many of the Jamaicans and U.S. blacks he recruited used the transport as a free trip to Panama, leaving Costa Rica as soon as they got to camp. In desperation, Keith imported Italian railroad workers who ultimately rebelled against the harsh conditions of the labor camps and refused to work. Their descendants founded the Italian town of San Vito on the opposite coast some seventy years later. When the French canal project ended in failure,

78

unemployed masses flooded into Costa Rica. But the labor shortage had already done its damage, adding years of delays and hundreds of thousands of colones to the price of the railroad. ⛫ More than the labor shortage however, incompetence added time and cost to the railway venture. Keith made entire grades and sections of road before discovering his planned route was impossible and starting over elsewhere. His peculiar energy and managerial skills ultimately compensated for the repeated starts, but an experienced railroad builder could have completed the line for half the cost in a quarter of the time. ⛫ Nevertheless, after Guardia's death in 1881, his successors continued to rely on Minor Keith. In 1883, they entrusted to him the task of completing the railroad he had been constructing for eight years. The last section of its track would traverse the country's most treacherous terrain, going over the volcanic ridge, across unpredictable rivers, and into the Meseta Central. The Costa Rican government could not possibly bankroll the project alone, so they sent Keith to Europe to refinance their loans. ⛫ He spent three years traveling between London and Costa Rica, hashing out a rescheduled debt with the Central American nation's creditors. Finally in 1886, Keith, along with several British investors, formed the Costa Rica Railway Company, Ltd., which took over the building of the railroad under several conditions. By terms, the company would assume control of the entire line for ninety-nine years after its completion and would get 800,000 acres of land adjacent to the tracks. With typical enthusiasm and such incentive, Keith started building as soon as he

79

returned to Costa Rica. In 1891, two years behind schedule and twenty years after the government's initial negotiations, he finished the tracks. 🏛 President Guardia intended his railroad to propel Costa Rica into the world, which it did. Yet the railroad's side effects also injected the world into Costa Rica. The formerly homogeneous nation now had an unassimilated black minority inhabiting its lowlands, and it owed many times its gross domestic product to foreign lenders. Most conspicuously, however, it faced a massive foreign presence in its economy—the lowland banana industry Keith fostered as Siamese twin of his railroad enterprise. During the years he worked on the railroad, Keith built the world's largest banana empire. 🏛 Like most Caribbean farmers, Costa Ricans grew bananas for local consumption. The fruit did not have many fans outside the tropics because no variety could survive transport—at least not until a Frenchman discovered the Gros Michael variety, known as the bomb-proof banana. In the early 1870s, Minor Keith imported Gros Michael bananas into Costa Rica, cultivating them on his own lowland holdings and encouraging local farmers to do the same. As his railroading provided access to a greater part of Limón's hinterland, he expanded his cultivation, nurturing a banana empire that combined his own harvest and that of smaller growers. In 1883, he exported 100,000 stems to North America, mainly to New Orleans. In 1879, he shipped the first bananas to reach New York City, and in 1890, he sold more than one million stems. 🏛 Keith invented the banana industry. Even the durable variety he grew could survive for less than two weeks after cutting, so he developed a highly organized system of harvest and transport that could successfully bring fruit to market. From 1882, he took advantage of the completed sections of the lowlands railway to bring bananas to Limón within hours of harvest. He then used Caribbean steamships to speed the fruit overseas. After 1891, as shareholder in the foreign-owned Costa Rican Railway Company, he cut himself a deal on banana hauling, much better than the rates given coffee growers on the Meseta. In 1898, Keith's produce dominated the southern U.S., but it ranked second overall to the Boston Fruit Company, which dominated in the U.S. Northeast. Finding himself in financial straits, Keith agreed in 1899 to merge with his rivals, forming the colossal United Fruit company, later renamed United Brands, a powerful force in Costa Rica and the fruit-growers' world to this day. 🏛 Although Keith and other foreign investors made a great deal of money in bananas, the industry had almost no impact on Costa Rica. Through corrupt deals with Tico politicians, Keith and his cronies paid almost no taxes. Because their workers bought mainly from company commissaries, banana money did not even enter the economy indirectly. As agro-exporters, banana interests naturally jibed with the political desires of the *cafetaleros*; nonetheless, many elites fought hard against the banana intrusion, against foreign investment in general, and against Guardia's railroading the country into debt. But these detractors lost the policy war, so Costa Rica entered the twentieth century with a huge debt and foreign-controlled lands.

🏛 🏛 🏛

V

The Middle Class Revolution

*M*uch as rural laborers took control of the French Revolution and urban laborers the Russian, the relatively small Tico middle class seized the reins of the 1940s anti-government movement in Costa Rica, creating Latin America's most stable democracy in the aftermath of the country's worst social crisis. Middle class predominance in the revolution occurred not by virtue of power but by strategic position. Politically, middle class Ticos stood as an acceptable compromise in the conflict between Costa Rican upper and lower classes, a conflict dating from the early decades of the twentieth century.

BETWEEN THE WARS

A scant 65,000 people populated Costa Rica when it declared independence in 1821; by 1927, there were nearly ten times that many. As death rates fell and birth rates rose in the 1930s and 1940s, the country's population exploded. Traditionally, agricultural colonization relieved population pressure and minimized the gap between rich and poor by endowing Ticos with land of their own. By the 1930s, in fact, much unsettled land remained to accommodate this rising population, but twentieth-century liberal leaders neglected to build roads that would give farmers access to uninhabited areas. So, in the first decades of the twentieth century, Costa Rica changed from a nation of farmers who held small parcels of land to one of laborers. By the 1940s, just five percent of the country's landowners controlled over

fifty percent of the land, and two-thirds of the population worked for wages either on farms or in factories. During that time, landless farm laborers poured into the central urban region. With wilderness less able to act as Costa Rica's social panacea, economic inequity became the single issue of public concern in the decades between the century's two world wars.

The Great War (1914-1919), or World War I, immediately depressed the Costa Rican economy, mainly because of an Allied blockade against Germany, Costa Rica's major trading partner. Deprived of lucrative European sales, coffee exporters had to compete in the low-priced American market. Tico producers survived by retreating into subsistence agriculture, but estate owners and exporters counted large losses. For the first time, Costa Rica suffered for its dependence on one crop. After the war, coffee prices bounced back, reaching a historic high by the late 1920s, but relative to industrial goods like steel, coffee slipped in value. It would continue to do so for fifty years.

In 1929, the industrialized world entered a depression. Although Costa Rica's favored position in the European market shielded it somewhat, coffee prices dropped fifty percent by 1933. To minimize its losses, the coffee class expanded output by increasing the area under production and cut the wages of coffee laborers, who already made ten times less than banana workers. Despite these measures, profits shrank further. The *cafetaleros* partly blamed their misfortune on the high price of land around the Meseta or the exorbitant transport charges levied by United Fruit, which controlled the Jungle Train. Apart from its usurious rail fees, however, the banana firm acted as partner to the coffee class, reinforcing its agro-export interests in the national forum. Both fruit industry and coffee elite favored a low, regressive tax structure that hit the poor more than the rich, and they fought together to maintain Costa Rica's traditionally open economy. They also mutually repressed non-agricultural industries like textiles that might otherwise have competed for their labor force.

Despite the agro-interests' struggle to maintain profit margins, the Costa Rican economy hit bottom in 1933. That year, the *cafetaleros* lost their financial and philosophical partner when United Fruit severely cut back production in the Atlantic lowlands. Coffee accounted for more than two-thirds of national exports; because of this near exclusive reliance on an undervalued commodity, the country's economy worsened. Not by coincidence, 1933 saw the oligarchy break from its staunch defense of laissez-faire capitalism to intervene in the coffee business, stabilizing prices and controlling production.

The Second World War, fought in Europe from 1939 to 1945, deepened the crisis for the upper class. Hundreds of Costa Rican export firms with connections to European roasting houses became obsolete, since wartime Europe could not buy coffee, and the entire coffee crop went to North America by way of U.S. importers. Wartime price controls imposed by the U.S. on all exported goods further stifled the Costa Rican economy.

Although the upper class suffered the most loss of status in this fallen time, in terms of real misery, Costa Rica's depression fell squarely on the poor. Many lower-class Ticos suffered from malnutrition. All cities, San José in particular, lacked sufficient housing for growing lower- and middle-income populations. Cramped living conditions exacerbated health problems associated with urban poverty. Inflation in the late 1930s and 1940s further impoverished the lower and middle classes by decreasing real wages.

The Costa Rican underclasses owed much of their misery to the successful repression of economic diversification by agro-industrialists, who channeled the country's financial and governmental resources into their own pockets to the exclusion of all other enterprises. The elites who owned the nation's banks carefully engineered the country's underdevelopment by extending credit to large agro-exporters of their own class, but not to small farmers or to industrial growth. With no prospects in the countryside and no industrial jobs, Ticos faced increased unemployment. Well-educated and articulate members of the small middle class had almost nothing to do; society offered few alternatives between working farms and owning them.

Yet, as Tico aristocrats typically pointed out, poverty in Costa Rica was not as bad as elsewhere in Central America. Still, economic hardship became increasingly weighty and unacceptable to common Ticos. Costa Rica's close association with Europe had always made Ticos aspire to that continent's lifestyle; in the decades between the wars, the gap between Tico aspirations and realities widened. At the same time, a high literacy rate made members of the lower classes less dupable by their "betters," less likely to ingest political palliatives. All in all, middle- and lower-class Ticos had the feeling that the upper classes had allowed the nation to fall behind in its standard of living, health, nutrition, housing, and infrastructure. This widely perceived upper-class failure compelled the underclasses to acts of political reform unimaginable to former generations.

COMMUNISM À LA TICO

Alfredo Flores became Costa Rica's first reformist president (1914-1917) when the country's Congress appointed him in order to avoid open conflict between rival candidates. Flores's progressive financial reforms incensed the elite, who were perfectly satisfied with state control that left the poor paying the most taxes. A group of aristocrats deposed Flores in a government coup, led in 1917 by the president's own minister of war, Federico Tinoco Granados. Plagued immediately by rioting Flores supporters, Tinoco's presidency (1917-1919) collapsed under further political pressure by external critics after the end of World War I. Despite President Tinoco's support of Allied forces during the war and his somewhat legitimate claim that he had not deposed even a properly elected president, his ascent to power did not comply with U.S. President Woodrow Wilson's plan to make the world safe for democracy.

85

86

The U.S. naturally refused to recognize the coup-imposed government and intimidated the regime with threats of intervention. A nervous President Tinoco imposed harsh military rule, especially in San José, and censored the press, a sacred institution since independence. As he lost elite support, Tinoco became desperate and even more obnoxious, sparking riots in all quarters of Tico society. Finally stepping down in 1919, he exiled himself to Britain.

In the early 1920s, various anti-Tinoco groups coalesced to form Costa Rica's first organized reform movement. The emergent figure in this period, Jorge Volio, had just returned from his European education, where he had embraced then-circulating ideas of Social Christianity. The movement encouraged Christians to improve the lives of the disadvantaged. As a young priest and son of the Cartagan elite, Volio himself, if not his ideas, seemed acceptable to the reigning oligarchy, and in 1923 he founded the Reform Party to run in the 1924 presidential election. Volio expressed desire for many of the reforms that Ticos would champion in the future: a progressive tax structure based on income, improved education, workers' rights, social security, agrarian reforms, and decentralized government. These measures proposed to cure society's ills without resorting to communism, which swept through similarly distressed countries only a few years earlier.

Determined to control the nation by keeping up the appearance of a constitutional democracy, post-Tinoco leaders widened suffrage to give the people a stake in the government, believing voters would side with legitimately elected rulers if another dictator grabbed power. Still, the leaders kept potentially divisive elements out of the public arena. Ricardo Jiménez Oreamuno, winner of the 1924 presidential election, offered reformer Volio the vice presidency. After accepting, Volio realized that President Jiménez had included him in the administration to suppress him, not to empower him. Taking the bait, Volio had been tricked into abandoning his own party. Thus Costa Rica's first reform movement died at the hands of its maker. Ultimately dissatisfied with his situation, Vice President Volio took part in a coup attempt in 1926, after which Jiménez deported him to Europe to receive "psychiatric care."

Having dispelled the reform party and its leader in one blow, President Jiménez (1924-1928, 1932-1936) and the next president, Cleto González Víquez (1928-1932), ruled the country for twelve years, alternating four-year terms. These Tico patricians, who had both held the office before, had the same anti-clerical, liberal viewpoints and ran administrations by and for the *cafetaleros*. Jiménez and González kept government to a minimum, greased the wheels of the coffee business, and maintained a laissez-faire economy, generally neglecting social problems. They retained power by carefully balancing mass popularity against *cafetalero* indulgence, an act that became increasingly difficult after the world fell into depression in 1929.

Any efforts made by these patriarchs to ameliorate the suffering of the masses came not from a heightened sense of responsibility but rather from popular pressure. Reformist sympathies were generated by the Communist party, also known as the Workers' and Peasants' Bloc, founded in 1931 by Manuel Rafael Mora Valverde. The party initially made headway only among young, urban intellectuals and laborers in the banana zone—groups susceptible to Marxist doctrine. To expand his appeal, Mora picked up the torch of Tico reform dropped by Flores and Volio; he also exploited the Tico habit of paying more attention to personalities than to party doctrines.

In general, Communist movements do not dilute their ultimate goal of revolution with reformist compromises, but Mora maneuvered as a populist, filling the then-vacant niche of reformer and shelving the idea of revolution. At the time, Mora and the Tico Communist Party leadership saw implementation of their ideology as secondary to improving workers' lives within the existing system. A native-born child of the elite, Mora conferred onto his party the traditional respect given a person of his extraction. As long as the people viewed Mora as just another charismatic Tico politician, his anti-capitalism neither threatened them nor took on an ominous foreign overtone.

The 1932 Communist platform proposed the workers' right to strike, an eight-hour day, and decent living conditions, plus agrarian reforms, women's emancipation, and state-supported expansion of infrastructure, agriculture, and industry. The success of the great banana strike that year gave the Communists a country-wide legitimacy and more influence with urban workers. While Mora's earnest and successful foray into Tico politics lost him the powerful mystique afforded a pure protest party, it also brought him great rewards. As the only reform candidate in the 1936 presidential election, Mora defined the issues of the campaign. Mora lost, but his party posted a viable contender in every subsequent race through 1948.

Tired of liberal patriarchs, upset by their own decline, and displeased by Jiménez's attempts to help the lowest classes at their expense, the Tico coffee barons ran a "heavy" in the 1936 election. León Cortés (1936-1940) won easily; once in office, he came down hard on the Communist party, barring Mora from his seat in Congress. President Cortés returned governmental control to the oligarchy, running a pro-German administration. He did so to appeal to the concentration of German immigrants in the elite . . . and because Germany had become Costa Rica's top trading partner. Having tamed Tico politics, Cortés backed his successor to the presidency, Rafael Angel Calderón Guardia, a politically cooperative pediatrician and leading lay Catholic who presumably would continue on the path marked by Cortes.

Instead of behaving as Cortés's puppet, President Calderón (1940-1944) rocked the nation by throwing off the programs of the old guard, initiating an era of paternalistic reform and taking away Cortés's Republican Party. Thus alienating his elite supporters, President Calderón gathered about him new allies in reform. To give all sectors a stake in his administration, he assembled a democratic cabinet, appointing advisors and ministers from all levels of society, and even brought in old reformers like Volio. Above all, however, Calderón wished to form an alliance with the Church. Happily for Calderón, both he and the new archbishop, Victor Sanabria Martínez, had been heavily influenced by Catholic social doctrine, which encouraged Church work toward solving economic and social problems.

Calderón needed as much support as he could get, because he advocated reforms more radical than those proposed by the Communists. He wanted a progressive tax system. He called for legislation that would allow squatters to get titles to land, and for other land to be redistributed to peasants. He asked for extension of credit to rural areas, funding for cooperative farms, and a national university. In his four years in office, he managed to effect all these reforms and more. He even gave shoes to first-graders to allay the social stigma of poverty and to prevent foot parasites.

Calderón's most important reform effort came in 1941 when he sent to Congress his Social Security plan, which inaugurated widespread government intervention. Based on a Chilean model, it gave the entire populace accident, sickness, disability, old age, and unemployment insurance. It also raised salaries, improved housing, and created health-care facilities. The plan concerned itself with the distribution of society's resources to the underclass without suggesting how to industrialize and develop the country or how to help the middle class; both omissions would prove costly, politically.

In the 1920s, Tico *campesinos* began migrating to the Atlantic lowlands to seek the better wages offered by American-owned United Fruit (currently United Brands). Paid less than English-speaking Jamaicans and given less prestigious jobs, they resented being second-class citizens in their own country. A Cartagan Communist named Carlos Luis Fallas, who had worked for United as an adolescent, returned to the banana zone in 1933 and easily organized the Ticos. Jamaican laborers already had their own labor organization—a chapter of Jamaican Marcus Garvey's Universal Negro Improvement Association—and resented the idea of sharing power with their subordinates who they also believed were inferior; British subjects, the Jamaicans had adopted the superior attitudes of their Commonwealth. 🏛 United Fruit used these racial divisions to company advantage. Though the Jamaicans had staged protests against "Mamasita Yunai" (Mother United) for years, they were always chastened with the threat of losing jobs to the "underclass" Ticos. In turn, Ticos who complained were reminded of their expendability. Fallas's brilliance came in bringing the races together to strike against the banana colossus. For months he organized in secret, by lamplight, throughout the Limón district, until he felt the workers ready to strike. 🏛 In 1934, his strike committee sent a list of demands to President Ricardo Jiménez and various company executives. The Americans immediately refused to

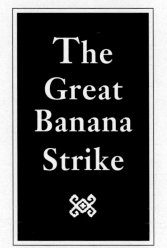

The Great Banana Strike

concede, and the next day, to their complete shock, ten thousand black *and* white workers went on strike, paralyzing Atlantic operations. The company tried its best to intimidate the strikers into submission or to bait them into imprudent violence, but despite inhuman hardship, the strikers held firm. To his credit, Jiménez rejected United's request to send in troops during the strike, having no proof that the strikers had become a threat to public safety. 🏛 After holding out for weeks, United agreed to work out an agreement with the strikers. The final draft equalized wages between black and white workers, raised wages in general, provided for better working conditions, and gave better terms to independent banana farmers. For his part, Jiménez imposed a nationwide minimum wage and personally guaranteed that United would honor the strike agreement. 🏛 The strikers triumphantly returned to work only to get tricked into violence by United lies. Company bosses informed the workers that Fallas, who actually had remained at the strike headquarters hidden in Limón forests, had instead reneged on the deal and escaped to the U.S., toting a huge payoff. The strikers erupted at the false news. Costa Rican troops joined United goons in squelching the disorder, which lasted for days. Many workers died, but their blood only cemented union resolve. 🏛 The great banana strike legitimized Mora's Communist Party and made common Ticos feel for the first time their connection to

90

the Atlantic zone, which they previously considered for blacks only. Fallas's communistic strike organization gave the party the mainstream appeal it needed to become a national political voice. Laborers in the banana enclave did more for the Communists than Costa Rica's coffee laborers did, because the former worked in conditions highly susceptible to Marxism. Common circumstances under a single employer united the lowland laborers, whereas the coffee peons' highly individual relationships with each of their employers divided them. Prior to the strike, Ticos had thought the Atlantic zone a foreign land and its black inhabitants strangers. When the strikers threw their suffering up to the national conscience, Ticos of the Meseta discovered a kinship with the Jamaicans, within a generation accepting them as full citizens.

🏛 🏛 🏛

By 1941, the war in Europe and the Pacific began to affect Costa Rica. A lack of imports during wartime caused a decline in customs duties, a major source of government revenue. Wartime construction projects, price controls, and employment projects made Costa Rican citizens perceive President Calderón's government as too interventionist. Despite the prevalence of German expatriates among his country's elite, Calderón declared war on Germany—just after the U.S. did—and came down hard on German residents of Costa Rica. He seized property from German and Italian immigrants, further enraging an upper class still reeling from social reforms. But the confiscations funded many of Calderón's social programs; he boasted of income without raising taxes.

In spite of the fact that President Calderón's enlightened reforms did not challenge the social system, his fellow class members fought him, seeing him as little better than a Communist. While the elite struggled against him, from 1941 to 1943 Calderón moved to consolidate his support by throwing in with the Communists under party leader Manuel Mora. The wartime alliance between the U.S. and the U.S.S.R. legitimized local Communists in Tico eyes, allowing Calderón to associate with the party.

The resulting Calderón-Communist coalition produced the 1942 Social Guarantees and Labor Code. The Social Guarantees formed a bill of rights for workers and commoners, establishing Calderón's reformist intent while upholding respect for private property. The Labor Code was

the controversial issue. Its more concrete guidelines, which put into law an eight-hour day, ensured a minimum wage, and guaranteed a worker's right to strike, upset upper-class employers.

The alliance between Calderón and the Communists enabled Calderón to use the Communist propaganda machine; in turn, it gave Communists access to legitimate power, hastening reforms they desired. Calderón toured the country with Manuel Mora in the 1942 congressional elections to counter Opposition propaganda. He also used Communist networks to disseminate information about government aid programs. The Communists actually suffered in the deal: by having legitimate power and by backing real solutions that involved compromise, they reduced the very tensions that a more revolutionary party could have exploited to gain favor with the masses.

In the 1944 presidential election, ex-President Cortés (1936-1940), the Opposition candidate, ranked high among peasant and elite voters. To compete for popular support, Calderón's would-be successor, Teodoro Picado Michalski, formed a "Victory Bloc" pairing Communists and Catholics. An odd political alliance, the partnership naturally stumbled when certain Catholics would not unite with Marxist anti-Christian dogmas. To pave over this problem, Communist leader Manuel Mora disavowed all the anti-Christian parts of the Communist doctrine, changing the name of his party from the Workers' and Peasants' Bloc to Popular Vanguard. Archbishop Sanabria then approved the unorthodox union,

even touring the country with Mora and candidate Picado to raise votes. The other candidates attacked the trio with anti-Communist rhetoric, but their insults did not stick because Ticos felt comfortable with their homegrown revolutionaries, and because international attitudes favored communism at that time. During World War II, the U.S. had trouble drawing South and Central American governments to the Allied cause since many Germans were part of the Latin American elite. Partly to counterbalance the pro-German element, and partly to reflect its own alliance with the Soviet Union, the United States encouraged Central American governments to cooperate with local Communist parties, who naturally favored the side of the Allied Soviets.

In such a convoluted political atmosphere, Costa Rica saw one of the most violent election days in national history. *Calderonistas* (supporters of Calderón) drove about, intimidating voters and stealing ballot boxes. Picado would have won anyway, but this violence tainted Calderón in the minds of the people. Though Picado won the presidency (1944-1948), Ticos fully understood that Calderón and his political machine in fact ran the show. In an example of the curiousness of Latin American politics, Calderón stayed out of the country during most of Picado's term, practicing medicine in America—yet he still maintained power.

After 1945, the Communist presence in the government counted as a large deficit for Calderón and Picado. The U.S. became hostile to international Communism, legitimizing the Costa Rican Opposition's anti-Communist stance.

Further disintegration of U.S.-Soviet relations affected Communist prestige. Party leader Mora was torn between commitment to the international movement and concern for public opinion.

Though limited, Calderón's reform efforts as president from 1940-1944 demonstrated to Ticos how the government could function as an instrument of change. He converted Costa Rica's liberal democratic state to a welfare state, pushing paternalistic rule as far as it could go. At the same time he retained the older social and political orders. Just as his predecessors in the old guard operated for the coffee oligarchy's benefit, Calderón operated for its preservation. Seeking to enfranchise the poor through popular reforms, he hoped to counter a Communist takeover and preserve his class status. But the upper class wanted to preserve its status as well, and reforms were delayed. Ironically, to defeat Calderón in the 1948 presidential election, the elite linked up with middle-class reformers that ultimately posed a much greater threat to their way of life than Calderón ever did.

DON PEPE'S REVOLUTION

In the background of President Calderón's 1940s reform programs, several power-hungry groups maneuvered. No group, however, orchestrated Costa Rica's 1948 revolution—the rebellion was the brainchild of the nation's greatest Opposition leader, José "Don Pepe" María Figueres Ferrer.

Born in 1906 to immigrants from Barcelona, Figueres

resented his parents' authoritative Catholicism. Bitter and searching, he traveled after high school to Boston and New York City, where he divided his attentions between social philosophy and hydroelectricity, a logical scholastic regimen for the aspiring leader of a nation with more rivers and volume of water per square mile than any other country in the world save New Zealand. In 1928, Figueres returned to Costa Rica and began a hemp-making enterprise on a remote farm, which he dramatically named La Lucha sin Fin (The Endless Battle). Powering his factory with water-driven turbines, he became the leading maker of gunnysacks in Costa Rica. He integrated other farming and manufacturing enterprises in the San Christóbal region with his own into a kind of cooperative. Developing the area along with his business, he ran in power and phone lines, built a school, and in many other ways shared his fortune with people in his employ. The people named him Don Pepe, "Don" (Sir) denoting respect and "Pepe" a simple peasant name that reflected his humility—a great attribute in Tico culture. His success as leader of the San Christóbal cooperative movement became legend throughout the country.

In 1942, the well-known entrepreneur made his first political foray in a fiery radio address against government actions associated with the July 1942 sinking of a banana boat off Limón by a German torpedo. Calderón and the Communists had organized a demonstration that had gotten out of hand: crowds looted shops and homes of local German, Italian, and Spanish immigrants. A few days later, Don Pepe

Figueres bought time on a radio station to denounce the government for not stopping the riots. Arrested mid-sentence and exiled, he became overnight a hero of the forces opposing Calderón.

Naturally, the traditional agro-export elite opposed Calderón. But throughout the 1940s they remained confused and divided. Wishing to return to days of absolute elite control and obedient peons, the ultra-conservatives rallied around former-President Cortés, who headed up the newly created Partido Demócrata (Democratic Party). Moderate conservatives backed the powerful newspaper publisher Otilio Ulate and his new Partido Union National (PUN), which advocated some accommodation of the underclass but wanted ex-President Calderón out of the picture.

The smallest but ultimately most potent voice of dissent came from the growing professional class. Denied a role in society by both the old elite and Calderón, the middle class strove to change the government rather than work for change within the existing system. Initially, this movement was articulated by two separate organizations, the Acción Demócrata (AD) and the Centro para el Estudio de los Problemas Nacionales (Center for the Study of National Problems). The AD, which formed the far left wing of Cortés's Democratic party, consisted of political veterans in their thirties who focused on political, not social, reform, calling for elections based on substantive debate, not on personalities. Although AD propaganda did not advocate revolution directly as did that of the Centro, AD supporters in fact were capable of realizing such an act, unlike the academic Centro.

The Centro began as an anti-Marxist, anti-*cafetalero* discussion group made up of young, well-educated, univocal, well-off males. Supposedly apolitical, the Centro from the start promoted the agenda of economic advancement for the middle class. Its supporters assumed the roles of passive social critics to mask their real goal—to take power.

Led by Rodrigo Facio, these young intellectuals wanted nothing less than their entire vision flung upon the nation; even more importantly, they wanted credit for the result. From its research into social problems, the Centro advocated many of the same solutions effected by Calderón—industrialization and democratic enfranchisement. Though they should have cheered Calderón's reforms, Centro members criticized him as a patriarchal reformer running the same old, corrupt political machine.

These three groups, the Partido Demócrata under Cortés, the PUN under Ulate, and the small collection of left-wing political reformers in the Centro and the AD, ran candidates in the 1944 presidential elections. Though all three hated communism and Calderón, they could not form a cohesive faction. Candidate Picado easily won. In spite of reform's loss at the polls, 1944 marked a turning point in the history of the Opposition. That year, Don Pepe returned from exile to become the driving force when the AD and the Centro merged into a formal political party.

As an expatriate, Don Pepe Figueres had plotted revenge on Calderón, joining the Caribbean League, a band of exiles willing to help him in armed insurrection. With other exiled Central American reformers, he laid plans for a revolution that would topple every dictatorship on the isthmus, starting, of course, with Costa Rica. Don Pepe received financial support through a single Nicaraguan rebel whom he had promised to help overthrow Nicaraguan President Anastasio Somoza after Calderón was deposed. Don Pepe timed his preparations well; after the violent 1944 elections, the idea of an armed uprising against Calderón attracted more and more Ticos. Ex-President Cortés had even written to Figueres in exile, inviting him to lead a revolt.

In 1944, Don Pepe helped merge the AD and the Centro into the Social Democratic Party (PSD). Under Don Pepe's influence, the party advocated sedition, vowing to overthrow the government and form a second Republic of Costa Rica. The nation's two other anti-Calderón parties, the conservative Partido Demócrata under Fernando Castro Cervantes (who took over after Cortés's death in 1946) and the moderate PUN under Ulate, wanted to dominate on the ballot, not the battlefield. In 1947, these three parties swallowed their ideological differences and convened the National Opposition Convention to chose a single Opposition candidate (Ulate) to stand against Calderón in the 1948 election. United only in their anti-Calderón stance, the National Opposition had to eliminate substantive issues from the 1948 campaign or risk internal disagreements that might tear apart the flimsy coalition. The new union decided on a highly negative

campaign against Calderón, to break his popularity with the masses. The campaign drove the populace into such a frenzy regarding election reform that only a National Opposition victory could have convinced the masses of a fair election.

While electoral reform provided the basis for Ulate's campaign, the Opposition message centered emotionally around anti-Communist propaganda. Running again in the 1948 election, ex-President Calderón openly campaigned with Manuel Mora, the leader of Tico Communism, as had President Picado in 1944. Before 1947, the Communist issue had provided serious debate, but during the 1948 election it degenerated into hysterical red-baiting on the part of the National Opposition. Ulate's newspapers agitated Tico *campesinos* (peasants) into Communist paranoia. In the final days of the campaign, full-page ads read, "Calderón is a Communist." Despite their proclaimed anti-imperialism, Opposition forces pandered to the interventionist U.S. foreign-policy campaign against local Communism.

In his own campaign, Calderón scolded his rivals for involving foreigners in national affairs. As it had labeled him a Communist, Calderón labeled the National Opposition unpatriotic, pointing out that it had all but invited foreign military intervention and created international doubt about Costa Rica's stance against Communism worldwide. Calderón argued that Manuel Mora was a local Communist and therefore belonged to the Costa Rican political family, not to the philosophy of revolutionaries seven thousand miles away. Unbelievably, in the middle of Calderón's

brilliant defense, Mora immolated himself by publicly affirming allegiance to the goals of international Communism. This contradiction of Calderon further convinced the masses that debate was impossible between the two seemingly irreconcilable political camps.

As election day neared, PSD leaders became increasingly revolutionary under the influence of Don Pepe, believing that, despite their efforts to thwart compromise, Ulate and Calderón would make some agreement and cut them out altogether. Opportunistically joining legitimate demonstrations for electoral fairness by local business owners, bank employees, and other professionals, Social Democratic goon squads baited the police, hoping to provoke a counterattack and thereby convince middle-class workers of the need for retaliation against the government. On July 20, 1947, this tactic finally paid off. Cartagan police brutally put down a white-collar demonstration in the city's central park beside church ruins. On July 21, police killed eight people. Local professionals immediately struck in protest, closing their shops and taking to the streets. National Opposition leaders in San José magnified the local imbroglio, using it to confront the government's refusal to satisfy white-collar demands for electoral probity.

The strike spread across the nation. Called the Strike of the Fallen Arms (idiomatically, a "sit-down" strike), it arrested all business and commercial activity throughout the Meseta. The lack of banking personnel hit the small country especially hard, since neither the government nor any private group held adequate monetary reserves. Fearing the strike would give the National Opposition control of the election process, Mora's Communists ascended from the Limón lowlands to stir popular resentments against the PSD and the strikers by dispensing food to people who could not purchase it from closed stores. Despite Mora's efforts to break the strike and Don Pepe Figueres's efforts to turn it into a revolution, the conflict ended through negotiation.

Several days into the strike, eight thousand women marched on the president's palace, vowing to stay until Picado agreed to give into the strikers' demands. They remained at his door even after the President ordered street lights turned off. Then, in the darkness, police fired shots, panicking the crowd. Humiliated by what seemed a premeditated act of cowardice, President Picado emerged from the palace and promised to settle the next day. Under such circumstances, the government got a very bad deal, forced to turn over control of the entire electoral process, including vote-counting and ballot distribution, to the Opposition. Satisfied that he had done all he could to seed insurrection, Don Pepe left San José for La Lucha to plan the details of his revolution.

Election day passed peacefully, but when the results started coming in, the Electoral Tribunal realized that it could not report a fair result because of disorganized and corrupt polling. A follower of Figueres had run the Electoral Registry, tilting the results toward Ulate. Candidate Calderón's supporters became convinced that the Opposition had corrupted the electoral process, and Calderón began to harden against

compromise. Ulate followed suit, writing in his newspaper that he would accept no negotiated solution. After long deliberation, the Tribunal handed down a decision in favor of Ulate. But in a fateful March 1, 1948, session, the Calderón-controlled Congress annulled the election results.

Don Pepe Figueres finally had his excuse for a revolution. On March 12, he sent thirty troops from his mountain headquarters at La Lucha to capture San Isidro de El General, the only city in the south with an airfield. Victorious, they immediately flew three captured planes north to collect munitions and foreign mercenaries from Guatemala, making rebel troops better equipped and greater in number than the three hundred-strong Costa Rican army. To protect the airbase, Don Pepe's second in command blocked off the Pan American Highway to San Isidro by setting up defenses on a bluff at Empalme. On March 20, the government attacked; outfought and out-positioned by the rebels on the ridge, it retreated. At the same time, Don Pepe's remaining troops spread out from La Lucha, taking control of the mountains and valleys between the Meseta and the General Valley. Figueres planned to maintain this position until he had enough troops and munitions to take Cartago and San José.

Buttressing these military maneuvers, Don Pepe fought an equally important propaganda war to counter domestic and foreign apprehension about his revolution. Through diplomatic channels, he convinced the U.S. of his democratic intentions. Through radio addresses, he solicited the aid of Ticos and convinced them that he fought a war for

progress, not for a return to the repressive past.

On April 9, hidden by darkness and fog, Don Pepe Figueres descended from the mountains with three hundred soldiers and silently marched past federal lines toward Cartago. Simultaneously, some of his rebels airlifted to Limón. Both operations came off easily. Limón fell within hours, and Don Pepe, who reached Cartago by April 12, captured the city by the end of the morning. Keeping an occupying force there, he deployed an advance guard to the Ochomogo Height between Cartago and San José and a rear guard back along the Pan American Highway. Once aware of Don Pepe's maneuvers, the loyalist Federal forces quick-marched north on the Pan American Highway, easily breaking through the rebels' rear guard, and met the Cartagan defense forces at Trejar. The resulting clash was the longest, bloodiest battle of the war, and the rebels won it. The war ended with a count of two thousand dead, only one hundred of these from the rebels' side. The numbers underscored the almost surgical nature of Don Pepe Figueres's operations.

Although Don Pepe had resorted to violent methods in achieving his ends, he also had performed a great service to his country. His efforts ultimately made Costa Rica the exception to Central America's typical "banana republics," whereas Calderón's idiosyncratic reform program had no value beyond its immediate effects. Without the middle-class rebels, the upper class would have crudely reasserted agro-export domination once Calderón fell from power, creating a typical Central American government polarized

between populist forces and an unresponsive elite, completely lacking means besides repression or revolution for resolving social and economic problems.

The easy part was over; now Don Pepe had to negotiate peace, releasing his absolute hold on Costa Rica in a manner to leave him as much power as possible. On the night of April 15, 1948, Don Pepe Figueres and Manuel Mora, whose loyalist Communist forces held San José, met at the Ochomogo Height to discuss the peace. Don Pepe ensured Mora of his intention to retain all ex-President Calderón's progressive social legislation and to respect Mora's Popular Vanguard party. Mora offered to join forces with the rebels to repulse the Nicaraguan federal troops, who since the beginning of the insurrection had stood at the border ready to support President Picado, but Figueres declined. Under great pressure from the U.S., which wanted a quick end to the conflagration, President Picado and candidate Calderón stepped aside. After receiving written assurances that the Communists would have full rights under the new regime, Mora ordered his forces to give up San José. Having settled with Mora, Don Pepe had yet to make his deal with Ulate, who possessed the legal right to the power Figueres held.

One of the few politicians in the world memorable for his actions, not his words, Figueres minimized verbiage, using carefully controlled, mythic images to punctuate the purposes of his regime. When Don Pepe entered San José on April 24, he personally transported Ulate from hiding in the countryside into the center of the city, not in a car but on

102

the back of his scooter. This act not only underscored President-Elect Ulate's dependence on Don Pepe's revolution, but spoke worlds about Don Pepe's humility and sincerity.

Under the terms of their agreement, Don Pepe's junta would rule for eighteen months with a possible six-month extension, then turn over the government to Ulate for his four-year term as president. This accord signified a dividing of the spoils between the middle and upper classes, led by Figueres and Ulate. To consolidate power, Don Pepe attempted to destroy Mora's lower-class constituency by exiling or executing dozens of Communists and *Calderonistas*—ultimately outlawing the Communist party altogether.

Although President Calderón had established a modern reformist state within an arcane patriarchal framework, Figueres proposed to stabilize reform by incorporating it into the state apparatus. Whereas Calderón's reforms had betrayed the elite and given handouts but not power to the *campesinos*, Don Pepe satisfied both groups by creating a bureaucratic state that, independent of politicians, would implement reform efforts.

Don Pepe and the Social Democrats (PSD) put their trust in the new constitution that created a liberal Second Republic, mandating total state control of the economy among other progressive measures. But Figueres had yet to pass the constitution by a popularly elected assembly. Composed mainly of President-elect Ulate's delegates, the congressional group completely rejected the rebel constitution, ratifying instead a slightly progressive version of the 1871 constitution. Despite the numerical majority of Ulate's representatives, the rebels gained some important concessions in the final draft. They enfranchised women and repealed laws restricting blacks to the Atlantic lowlands. They provided a clause by which Congress could create bureaucratic institutions, such as social security and banking, whose officers remained independent of the executive branch. Likewise, the constitutional establishment of a strong and independent judiciary, electoral tribunal, and tax collector all lessened the opportunity for the party in office to abuse power.

The summer after the revolution, Don Pepe Figueres announced the first of his economic reforms: nationalization of banking and a ten percent tax on capital. Previously, banking had provided the ruling class a way to direct credit and therefore growth. When the state repossessed this power, it turned the flow of credit away from the agro-export industry and toward the cash-poor middle class. In another blow to the coffee barons, Don Pepe turned the Institute for Protection of Coffee (founded by ex-President Jiménez in 1933 to serve the agro-export moguls) into the Coffee Office, which ensured fair treatment of small producers at the hands of giant processor/exporters. Figueres's junta also put a fifteen percent tax on banana company profits. To increase the power of the government apparatus over the power of any political force, Don Pepe gave the government a regulatory role in every enterprise in the nation, including electrical generation, dairy farming, and construction.

103

Before stepping aside for democracy, Don Pepe committed two important acts to ensure his maintenance of power after ending the junta: he kept Calderón's 1940s reform laws, winning over Calderón's old constituency, and he abolished the army. The eradication of professional warriors limited the exercise of raw power by a dominant group. Figueres did not abolish the army by words alone. With his usual flair, Don Pepe took a hammer and knocked a chink out of the wall of San José's Bella Vista fort, declaring at the same time that construction would begin immediately to convert the barracks into the National Museum. After eighteen months, Don Pepe dissolved the junta and handed the government to President Ulate (1950-1954).

THE NEW STATE

Having turned over the state to Ulate and his National Union Party (PUN), Figueres and the rebels formed in 1951 a competitive political organization, the National Liberation Party (PLN), which watered down the Social Democratic (PSD) ideology and reassembled the anti-Calderón coalition. Don Pepe pulled support from the new industrial and agricultural sectors that benefited from his junta's economic reforms. Similarly, he garnered votes from the lower classes, who saw him as the only reformer in the political field. On the strength of this constituency, Don Pepe won the presidency legally in 1954, after Ulate's term.

Before the 1950s, the Costa Rican frontier provided a means of survival for the poor; during that decade, under PLN control, the interventionist state took on this role, improving the lives of the underclasses. With each new social crisis, such as a lack of urban housing, the state formed another Autonomous Institution to ameliorate the problem. The Civil Service, created in 1953, was the cornerstone of the PLN's power. Don Pepe institutionalized the traditionally important education system, making it a large branch of the civil service, which provided a livelihood for the party's principal constituency—the urban middle class. School became mandatory through the ninth grade, after which students went to either vocational or academic cycles, then to the workplace or college. Aside from maintaining the country's high literacy rate, the system indoctrinated each new generation in good citizenship.

After Don Pepe's term as head of the nation and the National Liberation Party (PLN), the presidency went to a candidate of Ulate's party, the National Union Party (PUN). And, until very recent times, the office has continued, like clockwork, to alternate between the two parties. Although this odd political tradition implies an equal sharing of power between the two parties, the PLN has remained the dominant force in Costa Rican politics, partly because of its skill at controlling the Second Republic it had created. Critics point out that government reform programs provided palliatives for social ills but did not approach root causes, arguing that the state offered concessions to the dominated classes without enfranchising or empowering them.

In the 1950s, the leaders of the new interventionist state plunged forward. The first major challenge for the new interventionist state came from the countryside. Following the formation of the Second Republic, the frontier completely closed and the rural population boomed, further concentrating land ownership in a few wealthy hands and dramatically increasing landlessness among peasants. Simultaneously, agriculture mechanized and intensified, taking jobs away from newly landless laborers. The agrarian reform law of 1961 did not implement real agrarian reform but sidestepped it instead—the government purchased acreage from landed people and gave it to the landless. Since the government had to foot the bill, available finances strictly limited the extent of the program.

Stalled in its attempt at straightforward land redistribution, the government tried several other approaches to reform. The Lands and Colonization Institute helped settlers get titles to land they had already cultivated. The Institute also initiated colonization projects, wherein settlers could relocate onto remote virgin lands. Once established, however, these communities needed roads, phones, and other improvements, and the costs far outweighed the benefits of the program.

Having failed in its first outings, the 1970s government revitalized the colonization program into a successful support network of rural cooperatives, reminiscent of Don Pepe's pioneering efforts at La Lucha. Indeed, cooperatives make up a large section of the nation's rural work force today,

105

and account for much of Costa Rica's production.

Through all these attempts at change, the Tico peasant has had little voice in decision-making. Costa Rican peasants, though active in government-sponsored communal organizations, have never mobilized as a political group, resorting instead to individual protest, such as squatting. Many peasants perceive themselves as part of a group too diverse to unite on issues. Those with a significant bit of land think they are worlds apart from those with a tiny bit of land, who in turn think they are a world apart from those with no land at all.

Today, grassroots organizations begun by the government tend to contain, rather than direct, local movements and energies. The only successful grassroots movement of recent times, the nationwide electricity strike of 1982, succeeded in lowering rates only because housewives who did not participate in government groups organized it. Government programs slackened in the 1980s. While this increased the hardships of peasant life, it also encouraged independent peasant organizations that will ultimately have a greater effect on rural Ticos than all government programs put together.

The government dealt with labor reform as it dealt with rural reform: by using handouts and repression as needed to prevent successful organization. Don Pepe's revolutionary junta raised salaries for laborers yet outlawed Communist-based unions. Strong in the 1940s under President Calderón,

Catholic-supported labor organizations dissipated after the revolution, its leaders moving into Figueres's PLN. Costa Rica's strongly anti-labor employers and the state also stole wind from the unions with concessions like minimum-wage increases. Costa Rica's *solidarismo* movement, an alternative to organized labor that greatly favors management, further defeated unionism by emphasizing cooperation over traditional union concerns like workers' rights.

Solidarismo and other interventionist measures relied directly on the government's ability to pay for them and, in hard times, became difficult to finance. In response to the 1970s Arab oil embargo, the impoverished Costa Rican government scaled down the state's role as a problem-solver. Under a new law, the president could appoint or fire the heads of Autonomous Institutions, abandoning the intent of the Second Republic.

Despite these measures and drastic cutbacks in the 1980s, the government has not entirely shaken off its role as a social equalizer. In fact, it cannot, since the state gains much of its legitimacy through its social mission. Throughout the Second Republic, the upper and middle classes have been most powerful, but as the state becomes increasingly unable to immobilize the underclass with expensive handouts, PLN and PUN supporters may have to start sharing control. If this happens, the Ticos' strong faith in democracy will allow a change in political participation without revolution.

VI

Ecology and Wildlife

Before Costa Rica became part of the permanent land-bridge from North to South America, its uplifted portions formed an island archipelago between the two continents. Ecologically, these islands resembled the Caribbean islands at Western contact: they were dominated by seed plants from the south and animals from the north, such as raccoons, that could island-hop. Surprisingly, tree sloths from South America had managed to populate the temporary islands also. Later, when the Central American isthmus formed in the middle of the Ice Age, northern animals dominated, and species from South America, such as the opossum, the armadillo, and the porcupine, migrated as well.

Plants moved across the newly formed land bridge, too. Alpine plants moved from the North American Rocky Mountains to the higher altitudes of what would become Costa Rica. Mountainous plants from the Peruvian Andes spread to the north as well, but reached only as far north as the Talamancan range in southern Costa Rica. Eventually, tropical forest and the animals that lived in it—monkeys, capybaras (the world's largest rodents), agoutis (Guinea pigs), and anteaters from South America—moved in, replacing the island grasslands and putting finishing touches on an ecosystem that would see no significant changes until Spanish contact.

The Costa Rican tropical forest's famous genetic diversity derives from an abundance of food and consistently moderate weather, which reduces to near zero the natural pressures placed on forest inhabitants. Without environmental stress, species evolve by adapting different defenses against predation and by developing various means of competing with other organisms for favored resources and shelter. An animal under great environmental pressure evolves in less complex ways than does a creature of the tropics. A Canadian caribou, for instance, adapts to sub-zero weather simply, by growing a thick, bushy coat. In contrast, tropical butterflies evolve in countless ways to avoid being eaten by birds. These insects may eat a plant that makes their flesh distasteful, develop a coloring pattern that confuses predators, fly only at night to avoid most birds, fly in a self-protective flock, leave the female in a safe, semi-larval stage throughout her reproductive cycle, resemble a common leaf, resemble a distasteful butterfly, or merely reproduce in such great numbers that predators cannot eat every one. In as many ways, tropical plants generate methods to compete for incoming light. Lush jungle life means prolific numbers of species.

In such forest, the slightest shift in pattern can result in yet another species. For example, a species of bee that pollinates a certain nocturnal orchid only visits the flower between 12 A.M. and 3 A.M.; all orchids not in bloom between those times cannot be pollinated, and, thus, cannot propagate. Yet on one occasion, three orchids bloom accidentally at dawn and miss their bee pollinator. In most cases, such flowers would die without producing offspring. But, by chance, these few orchids get visited by a hummingbird that has the right beak shape to pollinate them, and they bear fruit. If this offbeat pollination

occurs faithfully for a few generations, this particular type of orchid will never again bloom in time for bees, but a new orchid species pollinated by hummingbirds will have begun. Because the forest ecosystem has extraordinarily tight tolerances, any perturbation of its established pattern will more likely result in the creation of a new species than in a behavioral change by an existing one.

NEW CONSERVATION IN THE COSTA RICAN PARKS SYSTEM

Since the first Spanish settlements in Costa Rica, systematic deforestation by farmers and ranchers has replaced diverse tropical habitats supporting millions of organisms with monocultures (single crops) supporting a few thousand people, or with pastures supporting a few hundred cows. The trade is not so even as it seems. Without forest to protect the soil, previously mild effects of erosion turn catastrophic. The nude land quickly loses topsoil and generates more runoff. In turn, swollen streams further erode their banks. As cities grow, urban developers pave over cropland, forcing farmers farther into the wilderness, increasing even further the costly conversion of natural domains.

The shrinking ecosystem is somewhat able to survive fragmentation by humans, mostly due to the ability of some birds and insects to travel between patches of forest. Nevertheless, deforestation creates an ecological problem beyond the acreage it destroys. Most of the rain and humidity in the forest comes from the plants themselves, not from outside precipitation. At some point, difficult for scientists to determine absolutely, a forest becomes too small to create a sufficiently humid climate for itself. These changes may for the first few years only lengthen a normal rainless period, but dry spells that would barely affect a North American forest wreak havoc in the tropics: streams dry up, bromeliads (plants that take root on trees) die.

Costa Rican environmental pressures have been exacerbated by the country's participation in the world economy. To increase crop yields and produce blemish-free produce for U.S. markets, Tico farmers apply pesticides—many of them illegal for use in the U.S. but still manufactured by U.S. chemical companies. These pesticides not only kill farm workers with residual toxins, but they also go back into North America on imported crops. Since so many poisons accumulate in the food chain, they also eventually kill wild species.

Until recently, Ticos attended these drastic changes in their nation's ecosystem with indifference, a cultural memory of an inexhaustible frontier breeding carelessness about land and resources. Costa Rica did not have even a university science program until the 1940s, when Rafael Rodriguez, a world-class researcher, breathed life into his country's ecological and biological studies by setting up the biology department at the University of Costa Rica. Still, through the 1950s, Costa Rican ecology and biology suffered from an apathetic public more interested in applied sciences and from university regents more concerned with turning out

high-school biology teachers than field scientists. Rodriguez's most important donation to his country's and to the world's understanding of tropical ecosystems came in 1961 when he began the Organization for Tropical Studies (OTS).

The OTS, a cooperative association of U.S. and Costa Rican universities, gives top scholars from both countries an opportunity to learn techniques of tropical field research. The exceptional diversity of Costa Rican flora and fauna in such a small area makes the country ideal for biological research. Within a land area smaller than Lake Michigan, Costa Rica contains hundreds of different ecosystems, a dozen life zones, and three types of forest: the tropical dry forest of the Northwest, some of the last on earth; the tropical moist forest, distributed abundantly throughout the country; and the tropical wet forest at the northeast and southwest corners. The OTS has educated a generation of North American and Tico tropical biologists—ninety-five percent of U.S. graduate students in tropical science have studied in Costa Rica under an OTS program. Tico biologists, for their part, have benefited greatly from the expertise of U.S. scientists and from participating in well-funded U.S. research projects. Native graduates of OTS programs now run the national parks program and the university science departments, with great understanding of natural processes.

Since its origin, much world-renowned research has emerged from OTS-sponsored programs. In the 1960s, the OTS field station at Rincón de la Osa (the corner of Osa) became the world gathering place for ecologists raising the alarm about rainforest destruction. In the 1970s and 1980s, Donald Perry, a California biologist, pioneered forest canopy research at the OTS La Selva field station in the mountains north of San José. In the same period another U.S. biologist, Daniel Janzen, conducted critical studies into the shrinking tropical dry forest of the Northwest. Due to the scarcity of the ecosystem, his research at Santa Rosa National Park has become the standard for all future work in that field.

Even outside the OTS, Costa Rica has nurtured important natural research and conservation activities. In the 1940s, the General Valley provided a home for the New World tropics' most famous ornithologist and philosopher—North American Alexander Skutch, who still lives without electricity on a farm outside San Isidro. In 1954, international journalist Joshua B. Powers founded the Caribbean Conservation Corporation (CCC) after reading Florida naturalist Archie Carr's account of his search for the nesting site of the green turtle in the book, *The Windward Road*. The CCC's seasonal monitoring of the western Caribbean green turtle colony at its research station in Tortuguero is the longest ongoing sea turtle research program in the world. Through the CCC's efforts, green turtle populations, endangered by commercial exploitation as an exotic food source and by ocean pollution, including plastics and oil spills, have made a recovery.

In modern times Costa Rica has become more famous for its conservation efforts than for its coffee. The Costa Rican government has tried bravely to preserve areas large enough to keep life viable. In 1983, Alvaro Ugalde and Mario Boza

113

created the country's national parks system, which, including private conservation areas like the Monteverde cloud forest reserve, accounted for twelve percent of the country's land area, surpassing the current U.S. park area of 8.6%. A virgin park system can thrive in a wealthy nation like the U.S., but in an impoverished nation, protected ecosystems become slowly destroyed by indigent poachers and farmers who take advantage of unexploited resources. This has occurred in most of Africa as well as in Costa Rica.

For example, the Corcovado National Park on the Osa Peninsula, which contains an archetypal rain forest—colossal canopy trees of almost uncountable variety with wide crowns and pronounced buttresses—always housed miners. Their camps fouled the river, and their hunting robbed natural predators of their prey. Eviction only temporarily solved the problem, while alienating the local populace and disturbing the local economy. Corcovado's example profoundly affected Daniel Janzen's attempts to recolonize Guanacaste pastureland with original dry forest in the 1970s. Janzen, a favorite child of the OTS program, made pains to incorporate locals into his conservation efforts instead of posting guards to exclude them. As grants expanded the area of Guanacaste parks, Janzen did not evict native residents but instead encouraged locals to work for the park and allowed activities that would not hurt the ecosystem. Grazing cattle, for instance, could help the jungle reclaim pasturelands since the cows ate tree seeds and defecated them where seedlings fertilized by cow dung could grow into new forest.

Expansions of natural preserves into populated areas have become commonplace as ecologists recognize that many processes vital to the survival of a complex ecosystem operate by necessity beyond the confines of a small park. Janzen found that in the dry season moths that pollinate the Guanacaste canopy trees migrate up into the volcanic highlands. Every year fewer moths make it to the mountains, because they cannot migrate over Guanacaste pastureland but need the shelter of forest to survive the flight. Without these yearly migrants, the dry forest would ultimately lose its tree population. To facilitate the moth migration, conservators of the Guanacaste Regional Conservation Unit bought up corridors of forest connecting the parks to the highlands, including many farms and ranches that lay in between. These combined areas constituted a functioning ecosystem, where alone the Guanacaste parks did not. Today, within the larger area, moth migrations and probably dozens of other vital but not yet understood processes can occur. By not evicting the farmers, the park service earns the help, not the hatred, of locals, essential to a healthy park's survival.

The Corcovado and Guanacaste situations set fine examples for the Costa Rican government to follow. On July 25, 1991, with the blessings of President Calderón (the son of the deposed 1940s president), the government organized the entire parks system into regional conservation units, based on the Guanacaste model, that together covered over a quarter of the nation's land area. Today, these units include areas of human activity, farming and even forestry, as well as virgin national parks. The Costa Rican parks system has become a life-sized experiment in finding a way to preserve ecosystems alongside a human population. One novel experiment began in 1991, when Merck, the world's biggest drug manufacturer, contracted with the Costa Rican government to divide royalties earned from drugs found in Costa Rican tropical forests. Under the terms of the agreement, Ticos employed by the government will collect samples from forest reserves and send them to Merck's research facilities in the U.S. for investigation. Any successful finds will be the joint property of Merck and the Costa Rican government.

The government's commitment to conservation makes education a top priority. In 1988, the Tico school system, in a joint effort with the World Society for the Protection of Animals, developed a humane education program for use in the primary grades, wherein special classes teach children basic concepts of animal and environmental protection. In 1991, President Calderón gave the project his full backing, citing it as one of the most important elements of the country's environmental commitment. No world government, including the U.S., has ever supported humane education so strongly. In this and other programs, Costa Rica has made itself an environmental prototype for developing countries and for developed ones as well.

HOUSE MADE OF RAIN

Of all the ecosystems on earth, the jungle resembles most the coral reef. Trees, like coral polyps, provide both suste-

nance and shelter for the fauna of the jungle. Life in both ecosystems comes and goes violently in vicious cycles acted out by producers, primary consumers, predators, and ultimately decomposers. Individual species depend so absolutely on one another that the jungle behaves in many ways like a single organism, with a skeleton of trees.

The forest before dawn lies as still as a cavern lake. The sun has not yet set in motion rivulets of wind that snake through the forest in the day, agitating solitary leaves. Humans walking in the rain forest can explore a single, horizontal dimension of this fantastic realm—the understory—which holds only a small fraction of forest life. The bulk of jungle organisms live overhead, in the domain of birds.

A vulture floats high above the forest canopy, motionless against the gray predawn sky, sensing with its phenomenal nose carrion rotting on the forest floor below. As it passively tests the air for clues to its next meal, the great bird overlooks with its sharp eyes the undulating surface of the forest canopy. The overlapping crowns of tall trees, intertwined by clinging vines, create a nearly continuous green roof. In sharp contrast to the ordered treetops, an opening in the canopy made by a fallen tree contains an orgiastic growth of vines and other plants taking advantage of the light. When illumination penetrates to the forest floor, seeds and spores of light-hungry species that may have lain dormant for years grow quickly to cover the irradiated zone. Cecropia trees and large ferns pioneer these so called "light gaps," but as they grow, they create too much shade for the vines and grass beneath. The shaded plants die, clearing the ground just enough for a canopy seedling to take root. In this manner, the forest reclaims clearings and spreads beyond its current border.

At sunrise the wind buffets the canopy, collecting moisture rising from the forest. Later in the morning that same moisture, in the form of rain, drops back down. The vulture, floating lower as the wind begins, feels the moist air rising from the forest canopy below, where other birds have begun to forage.

In all, 820 species of birds live in Costa Rica at least part of the year, both permanent residents and migrant populations playing an integral role in the ecosystem. Birds forage in four different areas—the canopy, the forest edge, the forest interior, and the pasture. Beyond eating and surviving, birds spend most of their energy molting, breeding, and migrating. Many North American birds migrate to Costa Rican rain forests after spring and summer breeding periods, residing mainly in the upper canopy and in light-filled gaps. Likewise, kites and flycatchers come from South America to enjoy the surplus produced by this bounteous ecosystem. Permanent residents differ from migrants in their complex behavior, engendered by the equally complex rain forest. Many resident birds and flying insects move upslope in the dry season to breed and downslope in the wet season to feed. Hedging their losses from fierce predation, they invest as little energy as possible in a single nesting. Permanent tropical residents also exhibit bizarre social arrangements—some

types of gregarious birds form flocks with other species for foraging and protection.

Birds, along with other higher animals like mammals, process relatively little food, and do not defecate or die fast enough to contribute that much matter to the mulch. These animate residents act as visitors to a vast cafeteria. But migrants and residents alike donate to the life of the rain forest in a vital, strategic way by dispersing seeds over a broad area. Along with some bats and coatis, ring-tailed relatives of raccoons, birds eat fruit from canopy trees then move far away to find other treats. Seeds dropped to the dark floor will never grow for lack of light, but if birds defecate while foraging in a light gap or along the forest edge, undigested seeds have a chance to grow into giants. In this manner, birds facilitate the healing of forest gaps and spread the forest domain, functionally preserving the ecosystem.

Resting for a moment, the vulture perches on the crown of an emergent giant, one of the forest's super-trees that shoot up as much as 190 feet, far above the continuous upper canopy at 160 feet. Of Costa Rica's twelve hundred species of trees, a limited number reach this emergent stage. The flowering, fruiting, defoliation, and refoliation of these monarchs and lower canopy trees coincides with insect activities, bird migrations, or mammalian feeding and storage habits. Angiosperms, flowering plants in the canopy and below it, offer energy-rich fruit to birds and nutritious pollen or nectar to insects in exchange for pollination. Generally, insects pollinate, and birds and mammals disperse the seeds. There are

exceptions: the northeastern oriole, for example, pollinates some trees that flower in schedule with its migration.

After sitting for a time, the vulture picks up a scent worth investigating and takes off from its perch to enter the jungle. Upon reaching the surface of the canopy, which seemed from above a continuous mat, the bird quickly finds a passage among the leaves and vines. Once inside, obstructions become more sparse, allowing the large bird to move with ease. In this and every other level of the jungle, light, or rather lack of light, determines what plants will grow and what other life will thrive there. Vines tangled around uppermost branches of canopy trees cannot survive in the shade below, so these start to give way to less light-dependent species. Although the vulture experiences a much higher humidity within the forest (around fifty percent) than above, it remains quite cool from the absence of direct sunlight. The humidity, which rises as the vulture dives, provides the only source of water for the plant life of this upper zone.

The wide branches of upper canopy trees drip with epiphytes like orchids or bromeliads. Literally meaning "upon a plant," epiphytes root upon other plants without parasitically exploiting their hosts, in this case the bare branches of trees. The species that can survive in this peculiar type of wasteland, include several types of cactus and resemble desert plants in their adaptions. Epiphytes cannot rely on rainfall for their water, so they have the ability to draw moisture out of the air and store it. For nutrition, they have developed roots that catch falling and floating particles of dust, moss, fungus, feces, and pollen. Lichen and moss among the roots take inert nitrogen from the air and convert it into nutrients. Once established, these pioneer epiphytes collect enough mulch to support other colonizers; ultimately, the bare branch turns into a canopy garden.

This type of growth does not occur on every branch in the forest. Animal canopy dwellers—monkeys, lizards, coatis—physically clear select pathways for use as a canopy highway. Other trees remain bare because their bark peels too rapidly to support any growth, or because insects inhabiting the tree actively clean the branches. Generally, however, epiphyte-laden branches serve the important purpose of maintaining a store of organic matter at the level of the upper canopy. Not only do other plants, insects, and animals thrive off the garden's produce, but many trees send out roots from their crowns along their branches to collect the nutrients residing there—nutrients that they cannot get, perhaps, from the ground.

Bromeliads, many species of which have become popular houseplants in the U.S., have solved their water and nutrient deficiencies with a single adaption. Broad leaves at the base of the plant overlap to form a water reservoir, and the animals and insects that get water from these mini-oases give the plant their nutritious waste. Costa Rica's spectacular array of frogs thrives in the treetop marshes created by these tank bromeliads. Tree frogs lay their eggs in the bromeliad reservoir, then hatched tadpoles survive by eating other organisms using the plant for a home—insects, other frogs' eggs, and even other tadpoles. In adulthood, the tiny frogs have no

Though every part of the jungle plays an important part, the many species of ants surpass all but the trees in their importance to the organization and processing of forest life. 🏛 Army ants, in one of the most well-orchestrated and well-attended events in every forest day, march through whole sections of jungle, eating every living thing in their path. From their bivouac under trees or logs, the ants emerge mid-morning and begin to search for nearby food sources. Small successes focus the attention of the colony in a single direction, and the generalized searching resolves into an organized column. The random direction of the day's raiding ensures that no one direction is chosen twice in close succession. Small workers form the spine of the column, apparently guiding its movement, and soldiers provide a protective flank on either side. The column extends in a straight line for about fifty yards beyond the bivouac. Then, at the tip of this line, the ants swarm in a widening circle of foraging activity. Everything in this circle must either move or be eaten. The first ant to reach a caterpillar, for example, latches onto its leg or torso to slow the creature down until other workers can catch up and bite it to death. The ants quickly dismember their conquest and transport its parts back along the column to the camp. At the end of the day, the ants return along the column to the headquarters, or bivouacked ants, including the queen, follow the column to a new home. 🏛 The disturbance generated by the raid creates a cafeteria experience for the many animals and insects that follow the swarming ants. Ant-eating birds light on branches above the column and scoop up both the ants and the escaping insects. Butterflies faithfully flutter behind the column, coming down to suck up mineral-rich bird droppings. Several species of fly follow the raid, waiting to drop their parasitic eggs on fleeing insects exposed from underneath the leaf litter.

Ants

claws or teeth to guard themselves against numerous jungle predators, so they possess one of two defenses: they either secrete distasteful poisons, or move quickly.

Non-poisonous frogs make colossal leaps from limb to limb and some can even flatten their rib cages to create demi-wings, which increases their air time. Besides allowing for some quick escapes, all this jumping and gliding disrupts their scent trail so that snakes and other predators cannot follow them. Other frogs have poison glands that secrete onto their skin some of the most potent alkaloids produced in nature. Upon contact with a predator's tongue these neurotoxins seize up the throat or create a strong vomiting impulse. So as not to be mistaken for their palatable cousins, poisonous frogs exhibit brilliant coloration—incredible patterns of turquoise, green, red, and aqua. Potential predators see these patterns and look elsewhere for their next meal.

For the passing vulture, however, the main source of color on this level comes not from the frogs but from the orchids. Hundreds of them bloom in the canopy gardens. Over a thousand species of orchids grow in Costa Rica, one the national flower, most occurring as forest epiphytes. The line between species does not lie in large genetic differences—in fact, many species of the same genus can hybridize successfully—but in extremely restrictive reproductive adaptions. Similar species avoid hybridization by flowering simultaneously with their own kind and out of synch with other species. For instance, Costa Rica's national flower blooms in March, whereas a virtually identical orchid species flowers

in October. Though genetically compatible, they do not produce offspring in nature, so count as different species.

Orchids maintain their genetic purity by developing highly specific relationships with forest pollinators like bees and butterflies—which can actually fertilize a few species at once without cross-pollinating even one plant. A fluorescent green orchid bee, with a tongue twice as long as its body, visits five orchids of five different species. One flower lays pollen on its head, one on its back, one its abdomen, one its side, and one its nose. When the same bee visits another individual of the first species, the female part of the flower touches its head to gather the pollen, the female part of the second species touches its back, and so on, until all the individuals have obtained pollen without getting hybridized. Butterflies perform the same specialized pollination service for orchids that have developed highly specific food incentives. Through their narrow proboscises, butterflies can only consume liquids, so the liquids they eat must contain essential proteins. To attract them, orchids must produce a nectar high in protein. Some produce nectar laced with alkaloids, complex chemical compounds related to morphine that certain butterflies use as building blocks of their pheromones or sexual scents.

Effective pollinators visit just a few flowers on each plant, then move on. Canopy trees often bloom synchronously in thousands of bright flowers that guide the pollinators between distantly spaced individuals, so they can more easily effect cross-pollination. The bats, birds, bees, and butterflies that frequent these mass-flowering trees define the territory

of each species by their behavior. Large bees and sphinx moths can carry pollen for eight miles, so play a critical role in cross-pollinating canopy trees, thus maintaining the diversity so crucial to the forest ecosystem. Each species of giant fig tree has a specific wasp pollinator, which also travels the distance between individuals. Ground-dwelling bees, which eat pollen, not nectar, forage from flowers at all levels, then bring their finds back down to underground nests, and so maintain the vertical distribution of various plants. Bad pollinators, like most hummingbirds, sate themselves on the nectar from several flowers on a single plant. Such a feeding frenzy effects only self-pollination, which like inbreeding in animals puts the plant at a distinct genetic disadvantage, its seeds having a much poorer chance of survival than those of a cross-pollinated plant.

Sweet-smelling flowers attract moths, scentless flowers attract hummingbirds, and yeasty-smelling flowers attract nectar-eating bats. Over one hundred species of bats live in Costa Rica, compared to only forty in North America. Insectivorous bats, like those of North America, clean foliage and forage for insects. Others eat reptiles and birds. Most important to the forest ecosystem, however, fruit-eaters (frugivores) distribute seeds for large trees, and nectar-eaters (nectivores) pollinate epiphytes. These two types of bat possess the largest brains of any bats in the world. In this case and many others, the rain forest canopy has produced the most intelligent animals of their kind: parrots (the smartest birds), coatis (the smartest raccoons), and humans (the smartest primates).

Paradoxically, the canopy has also tolerated the survival of a seemingly devolved creature, the sloth. Sloths number among the few mammals in the world, along with koalas, that survive on leaves alone, not consuming calorie-rich, nutritious seeds. The animals' characteristic sluggishness comes not from a lack of will but from a lack of daily calorie intake. Sloths survive by blending in with the background and by having tough skin and a thick impenetrable mass of fur, which like the inanimate canopy houses thousands of organisms like moss, beetles, and moths. If the vulture landed and sat calmly for a time, it could probably find with its sharp eyes two sloths hanging on the branches of a nearby tree. Two individuals only occupy the same area for the short time that a mother sloth spends touring her young around her territory, moving on to a different habitat once the child can make it on its own.

At about one hundred feet from the ground, the vulture approaches a lower canopy that closely resembles in inhabitants and structure the upper story, though far dimmer and more humid. The roof of this level produces a feast of flowers for resident insects. The insects in turn produce a feast for lizards, which play a vital role in clearing leaves of excess larvae that would otherwise defoliate the forest within a week. To protect themselves from the lizards, insects reproduce constantly and have short dormant cycles. Their prolific regeneration simply spreads a more sumptuous banquet for predators, and in this way the vicious cycle of

122

rain forest life turns faster and faster. Many insects, however, have evolved protections against over-predation, more subtle than mass propagation. Some butterflies travel in multiple-species flocks. Others have different colored over- and under-sides to confuse foraging birds. And the erratic flight pattern of a butterfly mimics the fall of a leaf.

As it descends further toward the jungle floor, the vulture gets distracted by a stench coming from the open neck of a hollow tree. The dead core of a tree trunk exists as a remnant of past outer layers and does not necessarily serve as a support. In fact, some species derive a benefit, far greater than the structural strength they may lose, from having a hollow center. Forest creatures of all sorts—termites, scorpions, bats, and beetles—take shelter in the cavernous protected space. The guano and dead bodies of all the tree inhabitants fall to the bottom of the hollow and create a nitrogen- and mineral-rich compost heap for the host tree. Not surprisingly, trees that cannot fix their own nitrogen from the soil survive better hollow than whole.

The hollow tree does not distract the bird for long, and it crashes through the trees of the understory to find a dead kinkajou. A member of the raccoon family, the kinkajou, along with many other plants and animals, makes up the jungle's night shift. Lacking predatory marks, the kinkajou most probably died of disease. The vulture rips into the corpse's slightly bloated belly, feasting with one eye wary for predators.

Suddenly, the vulture stops plucking at the rotten flesh

and flies skyward through the understory and into the green. The jungle holds many dangers that could have startled the bird, including snakes, jaguars, and in this case a species that emerged from the jungle canopy millions of years ago to become the most dangerous on earth—*Homo sapiens*. Two people have just come strolling down the trail by the kinkajou's corpse to explore the only part of the forest that most humans will ever see—the well-trod floor. The smell of the rotting kinkajou mixes with the reek of vegetal rot to putrefy the damp rain forest air. This suffocating smell makes the forest, already claustrophobic with its labyrinthian trails, low-hanging vines, and dim light, seem even more so.

For the humans, who have frightened the vulture and other large animals away from the trail, the rot becomes the most readily observable process in the forest. Although three-fourths of jungle life exists overhead, everything above ultimately falls groundward to support the life below. The one hundred percent humidity of the understory provides a perfect environment for decay. Termites, woodboring beetles, and ants atomize the jetsam, centipedes and millipedes consume the pulverized remains, and molds and fungi of every color complete the process. At noon, when the forest is rather quiet, the buzz of ants and beetles rustling the leaves predominates over all other sounds. From this evidence it may seem that death in the forest outweighs life, but one boot-scrape below the leaf-fall lies not a rich humus but an ungenerous hard soil. Usable rot, pound for pound, constitutes a tiny portion of the jungle's mass, much less than the compost in an evergreen forest. The lack of readily available mulch explains why the business of rot proceeds with such emergency—if decomposers do not instantly transform the fallen leaves into mineral-rich plant food, the trees will starve.

Only one percent of available light gets through the canopy to the forest floor, but that one percent illuminates the interior of nature's cathedral. As from the ceiling of a Gothic basilica, the light, sometimes shaded in greens and reds, comes seemingly from nowhere. The huge, buttressed trunks ascend columnlike into the grand spaces above. Even in a storm the understory retains its composure. The trunks of tropical canopy trees, some hard as steel, can withstand colossal forces. Buttresses, which extend weblike from the base of a tree about twenty feet, are the major structural element for some jungle giants. Ariel roots, which drop straight to ground from the crown, root in the dirt, then tighten like piano wire, also serve to anchor the tree in high winds.

Hikers wisely keep their eyes open for snakes. Costa Rica has some of the boldest and most poisonous snakes in the Americas. Some of Costa Rica's poisonous snakes inject digestive juices into their prey to help the digestion process; others inject potent neurotoxins. Generally, snakes keep down the populations of large mammals, leaving the rodent population to the ants, which eat baby mice and rats in their nurseries. The fer-de-lance, called *terciopelo* (velvet) by Ticos for its deep pastel colors, maintains its reputation as the most

dangerous snake in the forest because it has no fear of humans and waits in trees to strike. Bushmasters, rattlers, and coral snakes provide hazards on the ground. In the canopy, smaller but equally toxic eyelash vipers await. The most immediate danger to hikers, however, comes not from much-maligned snakes but from much-ignored biting insects, which carry a multitude of fatal and debilitating diseases.

As the hikers continue, their path joins a stream. Streams flow out of rain forests completely clear, with no nutrient or mineral content, because the efficient recycling necessary for forest survival creates almost no outgoing waste. Ultimately, the stream flows into the back of a mangrove swamp. Mangrove swamps not only support an ecosystem of their own but also provide a crucial breeding ground for marine life. Marine birds rest and nest in mangrove branches, and immature fish live among the roots until large enough to survive in the ocean. Some species abandon the outer sea to join the mangrove system, such as arboreal sea crabs that spend half their lives around the submerged roots and half in the mangrove branches.

The two hikers end their stroll in the rain forest — the ecosystem that developed their dexterous limbs and oversized brains. Much like the crabs out of water, human primates emerged millennia ago from their ancestral home to inhabit not just *one* other, but *every* other ecosystem on earth.

126

VII

Modern Times

The twentieth century has marked a terrific struggle for Costa Rica, as well as other developing nations. From the turn of this century, the value of Costa Rican exports has fallen in the world market, the nation's population has boomed, and neighboring governments have splintered into chaos. Throughout all this, Ticos have demanded that society and government change with peoples' needs. Since its political revolution, Costa Rica has made progress against modern dilemmas in an imperfect, halting, and unique way, in the manner of all truly democratic societies.

ECONOMY

Politically motivated groups have blamed Costa Rica's uncertain financial standing on one cause or another, but diverse elements have contributed to the country's recent economic woes. A bloated state apparatus, a negative balance of trade, over-consumption of imported goods, limited industry, colossal domestic and foreign debt, skyrocketing unemployment, and slowed agricultural production have all kicked Costa Rica further down a slippery slope toward insolvency.

This economic slide started in recent history. While providing a solution to the social crisis of the 1940s, the National Liberation Party (PLN) under Figueres partly promulgated the current economic crisis by shifting government support away from the agro-export industry and toward the non-productive public sector without supporting an alternate productive industry like manufacturing. Since 1950, the Costa Rican middle class, which forms the constituency of the PLN, has worked increasingly in the nation's highly advanced but swollen bureaucracy. These civil servants account for a quarter of the country's wage earners and form the most powerful lobby against government efforts to cut social programs.

At the time of the revolution, the nascent manufacturing sector promised to lead the country to new productive highs. Instead, it never left the ground. For a century, Costa Rica ran an open economy benefiting agro-export interests whose representatives could acquire goods and equipment without paying import taxes. Since this policy of absolute free trade had squelched the country's natural industrial development, Costa Rican leaders joined the Central American Common Market (CACM) in 1959 and raised tariffs to give manufacturing an artificial boost.

The CACM accord further jump-started industrial development by facilitating a manufacturing scheme called import substitution. The darling of 1960s development theory, domestic import-substitution firms made finished goods (like radios) for the home market that had been imported into the country at high prices. Such a firm could bring in raw materials (cloth, for instance) and capital goods (like sewing machines) duty free. They could then improve on the raw components (for example, by sewing) and sell the finished product within the CACM, protected all the while by high import tariffs. Import substitution was intended, theoreti-

129

130

cally, to inject the economy with the value added to raw materials during the manufacturing process. Ticos hoped it would employ their growing population and drastically decrease foreign exchange losses.

Unfortunately, the magic combination of import substitution, foreign investment, and protective tariffs did not unlock the nation's economy. The historically entrepreneurial coffee barons didn't put much money into import substitution enterprises, and small business owners couldn't afford to buy expensive equipment or raw materials, so the field was given over to foreign investors. Costa Rica had plenty of labor but little capital; import substitution industries require much capital but little labor. A tailoring shop, for instance, has to purchase expensive sewing equipment from highly developed nations, yet might employ only a dozen people. The government collects no tariffs on equipment and raw material but only sales tax on the finished goods and, because of incentives, next to nothing on the company itself. And such a business pays little in wages; most profits go into foreign pockets. Lastly, the work force receives training on machines that most Tico business owners cannot afford to buy. Overall, the benefits to the economy hovered around zero.

In 1969, the state gave up the open development approach and began to intervene directly in production. Under the Costa Rican Development Institute (CODESA), the government created or took over private enterprises—for example, the manufacturing of fiberglass boat hulls. CODESA took on the risk of initial business investments by providing technical assistance required for startup and credit needed to buy expensive equipment and build factories. By its actions, the agency broadened the nation's export portfolio, giving Costa Rica the basis for a fiberglass manufacturing industry as it sold boat hulls abroad.

In isolated instances such as the example just described, the CODESA plan worked. But CODESA never turned into the tinderbox for Costa Rican industry it aspired to be. When the organization entered territory uncharted by Ticos, entrepreneurs applauded; when it began enterprises that competed directly with existing private concerns, it heard jeers from the business community at large. Furthermore, CODESA's charter indicated that it ultimately would deliver control of created firms to private hands, but no CODESA firms were privatized until the 1980s.

The disappointing performance of Costa Rican manufacturing has forced the national economy to rely on primary production as it did a hundred years ago. Coffee, bananas, livestock, and other agricultural exports account for just under half of the gross domestic product, bringing in Western currency desperately needed to pay off debt. Through export taxes, these crops also support most of the government's operational costs. But agricultural reliance depends on the availability and longevity of arable land. Until the 1970s, agricultural production rose steadily with land expansion: the coffee industry boomed, sugar sales shot up following the U.S. embargo against Cuba in 1959, and livestock rearing for the North American market provided the fastest-growing segment of the economy. Once most virgin farmland had come under cultivation, however, production could only increase with irrigation or chemical treatments—methods too expensive for most farmers. In the early 1980s, just after the Costa Rican government had won the fight to implement a one dollar-per-crate exit tax, the foreign banana interests slowed production on both coasts.

Slowing agro-exports combine with restricted industrial output to widen Costa Rica's negative trade balance. The country chronically has imported more than it has exported, which has the net effect of shipping money out of the country. Rampant consumerism among upper and middle-class Ticos adds to the trade gap by increasing imports of foreign durable goods. To make things worse, the consumer, industrial, and export classes pressure the government to artificially prop up the value of the colón against foreign currencies so that imports remain affordable.

Since money does not grow on trees, Costa Rica has had to finance its trade deficit by borrowing from abroad in loans eagerly given by Western financiers. In the 1960s and 1970s, Arab oil magnates poured their fortunes into European and North American banks. The bankers quoted an interest rate to these depositors, but in reality had nowhere to invest such large sums—until they thought of lending the money at profitable rates to developing countries. Enthusiastic lenders and international aid organizations encouraged countries to borrow, and soon the banks had driven Costa Rica and the

rest of the developing world into impossible debt.

In the red, Costa Rica has had to borrow even more to service its existing debt, and these service loans come with strings attached. The International Monetary Fund (IMF) and the World Bank favored economic plans that got money flowing into Costa Rica regardless of consequences, instead of encouraging Costa Rica to develop its domestic economy and then proceed to earn money to pay foreign debt.

Simultaneously, domestic debt and unemployment have created a startlingly vicious recessionary cycle in Costa Rica. From a countryside saturated with agricultural workers, Costa Ricans have flooded into the central cities looking for work. Lacking a labor-intensive manufacturing industry, the cities cannot provide full employment. Migrants either work for the government, remain unemployed, or enter the low-wage service sector—serving fried chicken, selling shoes. Adding workers to bureaucratic payrolls and unemployed people to the welfare roster increases government debt. This domestic debt creates a credit squeeze within the country, since the government must borrow some percentage of banks' available funds; the number sometimes approaches eighty percent. Unable to get loans, businesses cannot expand, thus causing more unemployment, which in turn increases the strain on social welfare, which increases government borrowing, and on and on.

The Crash

In the past few decades, Costa Rica's economic weaknesses

have brought the country to the brink of disaster, several factors pushing toward crisis by the 1980s. In the 1970s, recession in the developed world reduced export profits from coffee and bananas, the twin supports of the national economy. The 1979 Nicaraguan revolution closed off land-based trade between Costa Rica and northern Central America. Oil price increases in 1973 and 1979 drastically widened the country's trade deficit. Then, in 1980, President Carazo released the colón from its artificially high position and let it float in the world market. Inflation ran down the value of the colón from nine to thirty-nine colones per U.S. dollar. This rapid devaluation triggered action by both Ticos and foreigners who took money out of the country, causing an acute credit crunch.

Costa Rica's foreign debt, $1 billion in 1976, had risen to $3.5 billion by the summer of 1981, when under extreme financial pressure the government defaulted on all its commercial loans. For the next several years, the just-elected President Monge negotiated with the IMF to refinance the debt. Costa Rica became even more than before a ward of the IMF, which gave the country deadlines to downscale its bureaucracy, increase its exports, and reduce its imports. Despite Costa Rica's constant failure to meet such demands, the IMF continued its support partly because Western finance had fallen into a quiet crisis of its own. If kept to payment schedules, the debtor nations necessarily would default on their loans; if debtors defaulted simultaneously, they could bring about the collapse of the Western banking system.

Banking institutions survived by perpetually renegotiating loans in a shell game that kept the pretense of financial solidity over a facade of desperation. Lender institutions scrambled to get as much money back as they could, and make better loans elsewhere.

The so called Monge Miracle of bringing the country back to relative financial health owed less to the president's negotiations with the IMF than to those with his own people. The austerity measures Monge enforced could have been interpreted as a violation of the government's sacred social pact, but Monge pulled off a public relations coup that made Ticos temporarily sacrifice and like it. By 1985 inflation had dropped into the teens and the Costa Rican economy had started to grow again.

Our North American Cousins

International Monetary Fund support certainly helped the country back on its feet, but Costa Rica's real recovery began only after a bizarre, politically tainted bailout by the United States. Through the U.S. Agency for International Development (USAID), the U.S. lent and gave outright money to Costa Rica in exchange for assisting the Contra movement against Nicaragua, drawing a peaceful nation into war for moderate amounts of aid. Getting up to $200 million a year had a dramatic affect on the relatively small Costa Rican economy, propping up its international debt and enabling the maintenance of acceptable living standards while the country recovered.

135

136

In patriarchal, literally "father-ruled," cultures, the most liberated, independent phase of a woman's life begins at her widowhood or divorce. Then, she no longer falls under the protection and control of a husband or a father and feels no social pressure to marry, as she did in her youth. She can enter society as an unfettered and unfetterable individual. Not sur‑prisingly, in such cultures, widows and divorcees rarely remarry, having no reason to do so and many reasons not to. Historically in Costa Rica, the widow remarriage rate comes close to zero, one sign among many of the country's strong paternalism. 🏛 For modern Ticas, greater indepen‑dence and opportunity doubtlessly have lessened this absolute resistance to remar‑riage. But now, as always, women remain subordinate to the men around them, restricted in part by the national myth of womanhood. Costa Ricans believe that a woman possesses inherent moral and spiritual superiority, which she demonstrates by suffering and denying herself for her family. Mundane ambition or intellectual attainment would sully her purity, so in all practical affairs she must submit to the absolute authority of men. 🏛 Practically though, the predominance of men has never been absolute. Before coffee, women performed functions and created prod‑ucts crucial to the entire community, not just to their families. But money from the agro-export boom brought imported con‑

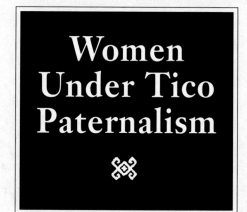

Women Under Tico Paternalism

sumer goods, making mostly-female home industries obso‑lete. At first, displaced women elevated their economic value with well-paid partial employment in coffee agriculture. This supplementary worth soon became women's only measure. The prevailing capitalist philosophy assigned zero value to unpaid labor, which included all woman's work outside the limited coffee industry. While post-coffee society continued to demand traditional labor from women, the economic system deemed their labor valueless. 🏛 Exploited by this differ‑ence between economic and social values, Ticas increased their power in society by educating themselves and by participating in their country's political struggles. Efforts in these directions converged in the 1918 teachers' demon‑stration against the oppressive Tinoco dictatorship. A year into the Tinocos' repressive reign, some teachers, mainly women, led a demonstration through San José that ended in the arson of a pro-government newspaper press. The Tinocos sent soldiers against them, firing into the U.S. consulate where some had fled. The bravery of the demonstrators and the gutless retaliation of the government troops galvanized Costa Rican resistance, and, soon after, the congress banished the Tinocos to Europe. 🏛 Women's movements have often resolved unorganized masses into a cogent, powerful opposi‑tion. The 1917 Woman's Day demonstration began the

Russian Revolution, and the women's march on Versailles brought down the French monarchy for good. Yet only women who feel enfranchised in some way take to the streets. Sixty years earlier, these Costa Rican teachers would have burned votary candles in church instead of a city block. 🏛 Unfortunately, the greater female enfranchisement in Costa Rica promised by this event has been fulfilled only in part. Although the country's 1949 constitution gives women the rights of citizenship and suffrage, women hold little real power and have formed no permanent political organizations through which they could achieve some. The constitution goes as far as declaring, "All men are equal before the law" (the word "men" apparently meant to include women as well), but despite these assertions of equality, family law has until recently handicapped women. Through the political action of women like Marguerita Arias, ex-President Oscar Arias's wife, Costa Rica has become the second nation in the world, after Norway, to give women equal rights under the law. And with Marguerita Arias running for president in 1994, the situation for Costa Rican women may dramatically improve in the future. 🏛 In other ways, also, Costa Rica's traditional homosocial society (in which women only interact with women and men with men) has relaxed, giving women inroads to a previously impenetrable world. Many middle- and upper-class Ticas develop careers, and partly because of this economic independence, come less under the control of the men around them. A wide acceptance of birth control, unusual for a predominantly Catholic country, helps women control

childbearing as well as finances. Even the financially and reproductively independent feel old social constraints, but life has changed for many well-off Ticas. Life for poor women, on the other hand, has changed very little. 🏛 Peasant and working-class Ticas find their lives limited by the same conditions that limited their great-grandmothers. More so than in the wealthier classes, poor women and men live completely separate existences. Women spend all their time in the home, at church, or at chores; men spend all their time at work or in the cafes. Many poor women avoid marriage altogether, opting instead for a monogamous, consensual union. Rural communities accept such couples, much as Costa Rican society in general has had to accept the woman's voice in her choice of sexual partners. 🏛 A few generations ago, families literally confined the dating and courtship of their daughters to the living room of the family home. Eligible at sixteen and an old maid at twenty-five, a woman found this brief span in her life to be the focus of great attention. Today's Tica chooses her own partners, but the super-awareness of adolescent girls remains a strong element of Costa Rican culture. Tour promoters celebrate their exceptional beauty; on the street, the women themselves seem aware of their special status. The typical image of the Costa Rican woman—young, doe-eyed, smiling—contrasts sharply with reality. Ticas are teachers in a nation that celebrates its educational system, bureaucrats in a government famed for its social services, and laborers in a country proud of its work ethic.

138

139

140

Of course, the money came with strings attached, strings pulled by a much more demanding group than the IMF. USAID pressed for cuts in the public sector, mainly achieved by curtailing social programs and turning over functions such as electrical power generation to private firms. The U.S. also insisted on lowering import taxes for U.S. goods and redirected the Tico economy toward exporting for the world market.

Most USAID money serviced Costa Rica's foreign debt, and the rest went to private firms in the form of grants. Since almost no money went into government-run development programs, USAID bypassed the Costa Rican government, denying it a voice in its own nation's recovery. Eventually, USAID came under fire for trampling on Costa Rica's sovereignty. Critics accused USAID of creating a parallel state redundant to and in defiance of the constitutionally constructed Costa Rican government. Indeed, through grants, it had supported education, construction, and investment projects seemingly competitive to existing public sector organizations.

When Oscar Arias became Costa Rica's president in 1986, he began carefully to disempower USAID. His smallest dissensions brought sharp and immediate reprisals from Washington, D.C., which withheld multimillion-dollar aid packages to punctuate its displeasure. Arias continued on course, however, ultimately bringing capitulation when USAID turned over control of its resources to the properly elected government. Ultimately, Washington had to back

down, but, as it did, it severely curtailed aid to Arias's Costa Rica.

Arias had won back his country's sovereignty, but at the end of his term he left the country with the same problems that had brought it to crisis. In 1990, Costa Rica had a $600 million trade deficit and a $4.5 billion debt, which accounted for ninety-six percent of its Gross Domestic Product. And the recession, combined with foreign-imposed austerity measures, had impoverished the Costa Rican people, further threatening the political stability of the most stable country in Latin America.

Ultimately, Arias's foreign policy victories paid dividends on the domestic front as well. The prolonged Nicaraguan war had limited foreign investment and tourism, stunting Central American economic recovery. Arias's pacification of the region brought back foreign investment and tourist dollars desperately needed to boost the economy. Although in the early 1990s foreign investors favored Mexico, El Salvador, and Argentina over Costa Rica, this lack of outside interference may allow a generation of Costa Rican-educated economists to control their country's affairs.

OUR CENTRAL AMERICAN COUSINS: FOREIGN AFFAIRS

Ticos share an attitude of racial, intellectual, cultural, and political superiority to their Central American neighbors. Such ideas led to disunity in the nineteenth century and an aloofness from Isthmian affairs in the twentieth. From 1903 (when the United States began serious attempts to build a canal through the area) to the present, Tico diplomats have mainly concerned themselves with limiting U.S. interference and officially maintaining their country's neutrality in regional conflicts. There are, of course, some major exceptions.

Early in the twentieth century, usually aloof Costa Rica participated in the ill-fated nonrecognition policy, which lasted from 1907 to 1934. In an attempt to discourage military coups, the Central American republics, along with the U.S. and Mexico, signed treaties in 1907 and again in 1923 to withhold diplomatic recognition of governments set up by revolution. The policy did nothing to deter revolts, but did severely destabilize foundling regimes. When a revolutionary government persisted despite diplomatic isolation, it was overthrown by North American intervention: for example, U.S. warships standing off Limón toppled Costa Rica's Tinoco dictatorship (1917-1919), and U.S. Marines spent nearly a quarter century in Nicaragua ostensibly to depose non-recognized governments and uphold legitimate ones. Finding that the constant U.S. presence did not stabilize the area enough to warrant foreign interference in their affairs, in 1934 Ticos led a successful fight to abolish the non-recognition policy. Since that time, Ticos have espoused an independent foreign policy hostile to dictators and friendly to the rebels against them.

Nicaragua

Since 1824, Nicaraguans have harbored some bitterness over Costa Rica's annexation of Nicoya (now Guanacaste province), an area long in dispute between the two nations, resulting in dozens of border conflicts. This old antagonism, begun when royal decrees in the year 1573 redrew national boundaries, heated up after Don Pepe Figueres's revolution. Don Pepe promised Caribbean rebel groups that he would help overthrow Nicaraguan dictator Tacho Somoza. Aware of the plans, Somoza supported two counterrevolutionary strikes mounted against Costa Rica in 1948 and 1955. With official U.S. help, President Figueres repulsed the invaders. Ironically, U.S. Central Intelligence Agency (CIA) operators, who thought Figueres a troublemaker, had helped organize the attacks against Costa Rica in the first place. The antagonism between the two countries reflected both personal rivalry between Figueres and Somoza and a widening ideological gap between the two governments. In 1953, Tacho Somoza's Latin machismo got the best of him, and he challenged Don Pepe to a duel.

Tacho's death in 1957 normalized relations between Nicaragua and Costa Rica. Following the 1959 Cuban revolution, the U.S. government, including the CIA, began to appreciate Figueres as the leader of the Caribbean, non-communist left, thinking of him as a front line against communism. Tacho's son, Tachito Somoza, took control of Nicaragua after 1967. Costa Rica maintained friendly relations with the dictator

142

Ever since 1830, when Costa Rica got its first printing press, newspapers have played an important part in Costa Rican life. The highly literate population (ninety-three percent literate in 1990) has grown with its free press, Ticos' ideas about their government and their culture developing on the pages of the dailies. The press also played a crucial role in the 1948 revolution. Contestants for power—the Communists, Ulate, and the Social Democrats— each distributed a newspaper that argued their side of the national debate. Candidate Ulate, a publisher by trade, ran the most respected Costa Rica daily of the time, *Diario de Costa Rica*. Ulate's profession and the continued connection between his PUN party and the nation's newspapers has lasted in what seems an undemocratic situation today, wherein the rightist PUN dominates the national press. 🏛 *La Nación* and the other national dailies have a pronounced conservative bias. Professional Tico journalists maintain strong ties to the PUN, and editors openly participate in political groups—unethical in most journalistic circles. Some national press executives even took part in Contra operations. This unabashed partisanship leads to stilted coverage in the press, an absurd news day occurring when President Oscar Arias (1986-1990) received the Nobel Peace Prize. On December 10, 1987, *La Nación* published a sarcastic poem and a banner-page article about a Costa Rican physician whose participation in an international organization called Physicians against Nuclear War had earned him a joint Nobel Peace Prize a few years before, clearly communicating the sentiment that Arias's international fame won him no favors at home. This kind of sniping characterizes *La Nación's* practice of free press à la Tico.

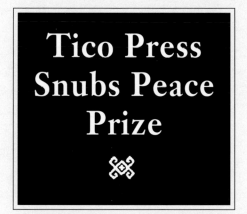

Tico Press Snubs Peace Prize

143

🏛 🏛 🏛

until he began to rule with arbitrary violence in the late 1970s. When northern Costa Rica became the home for the Sandinistas, Ticos of all classes and political convictions aided rebels against Somoza's dictatorship with seemingly patriotic zeal. Under National Liberation Party (PLN) President Daniel Oduber Quirós (1974-1978) and National Union Party (PUN) President Carazo (1978-1982), Costa Rica also led a diplomatic campaign against Tachito Somoza. Private citizens—with government cooperation—went even further, running a munitions pipeline to revolutionaries in the north. The Sandinista rebels who had found shelter on Costa Rican soil took over the government of Nicaragua on July 19, 1979.

Contras

Ticos in Costa Rica celebrated the ousting of Somoza, but the strict communist program of the Sandinista government soon dampened their enthusiasm. Disappointed with their new regime, many ex-Sandinistas returned to Costa Rican exile, including Edén Pastora Gómez, the Sandinista leader at the Costa Rican front in the war against Somoza. In 1981, Pastora, with the help of the CIA, set up an anti-Sandinista resistance force along Costa Rica's northern border. In its plan to overthrow the Nicaraguan government, U.S. intelligence counted Pastora's troops with the stragglers from Somoza's defeated army who had fled north to Guatemala and Honduras, referring to the combined effort as the "Contra" movement.

Though Costa Ricans in general did not back the Contras as they had the Sandinistas, Tico landowners in northern Costa Rica with ties to Nicaraguan conservatives aided the rebels. Aside from these Ticos, many conservative Nicaraguans, Americans, and Cubans sympathetic to the Contras owned land in Guanacaste. Tachito Somoza himself had owned thousands of acres in the region, until the 1970s when the Tico government confiscated it.

Outside the country, the Contras found a major supporter in the new U.S. president, Ronald Reagan (1980-1988). U.S. policy makers wanted to heap aid on the fighters in northern Costa Rica, but for the world community to accept a U.S. initiative to overthrow a sovereign government, Reagan needed the moral support of the Costa Rican government. Generally, Ticos did not consider the Sandinista government a dictatorship, so did not want to support rebels against it. But Costa Rica's deep economic depression gave the Reagan administration a tool to turn the Tico government to an overt anti-Sandinista stance. In direct exchange for huge aid packages, President Alberto Monge (1982-1986) tolerated Contra activities within his country's northern border, rejected area peace plans that did not jibe with U.S. objectives, and legitimized Reagan's aid to the Contras with appearances in Washington.

In aiding the anti-Sandinista military movement in northern Costa Rica, the U.S. militarized a formerly pacifist country. Starting in 1979, the U.S. assisted Ticos in modernizing their neutral civil and rural guards into a modern army, creating the strange situation where a non-army of a neutral country became an army for an allied country.

In the mid 1980s, the players in the Costa Rican Contra movement changed dramatically. In 1984, the U.S. Congress outlawed all funding to the Contras. Lacking official sanction, CIA field workers withdrew and less stable elements under Lieutenant Colonel Oliver North took over the U.S. aid efforts. In 1985, a rightist Contra group got rid of the moderate Edén Pastora because they had tired of the ex-Sandinista's monopolizing the northern Costa Rican front. With Pastora out of the picture, mercenaries with private U.S. backing took over the Costa Rican Contras. Many of these were foreigners just as eager to profit from gun running and drug smuggling as to overthrow Nicaraguan officials. Cognizant of the Contras' corruption, U.S. President Reagan's administration nonetheless directed Oliver North to coordinate U.S. fundraising and provide the new Contras a link to U.S. intelligence. The rebels staged terrorist attacks and bombings all over Costa Rica, blaming them on the Sandinistas in order to turn Tico opinion.

Since the mid-1970s, Costa Rica's involvement in military actions against Nicaraguan governments, first Somoza's then the Sandinistas', deeply bruised the democracy's moral authority as a neutral "Switzerland of Central America." President Oscar Arias (1986-1990), who had entered office cool toward Contra efforts, aimed to restore Costa Rica's impartiality. Arias could stand up to the U.S. because of his own country's economic improvement and because

corruption involving the funding of the Contras (the U.S. Iran-Contra scandal in 1986) had embarrassed the Reagan administration. His first year in office, Arias sent uncorrupted legions of the Civil Guard to shut down Contra air bases in the north. Later that year, Arias visited Washington, D.C., for the first time as president and delivered a deliberate speech to the U.S. Congress about promoting peace, not war.

Oscar Arias's Peace Plan

In 1987, President Arias drafted a peace plan for the Central American region that recognized the legitimacy of all ruling regimes, including the Sandinistas, and called for regional leaders to enforce cease-fires and give amnesty to all anti-government rebels. By recognizing the Sandinistas, Arias flew in the face of U.S. President Reagan's foreign policy goal of destabilizing the Nicaraguan government. Despite Reagan's objections, all five Central American presidents signed Arias's peace accord in August 1987.

The peace plan delineated a mechanism for creating democratic societies in Central America by bringing all unarmed opposition groups into open dialogues and encour-

aging popular political participation. Granting amnesty to rebels, it allowed them to enter into a constructive opposition. It mandated free elections with a free press. Those who signed had to stop assisting revolutionary forces while requesting the U.S. and Cuba to do so as well, and not permit their border territories to serve as launching points for revolutions.

In October 1987, Arias won the Nobel Peace Prize. The extra publicity given the accord changed the world's view of Central America. Instead of conceptualizing area conflicts as incidents in the global struggle between East and West, the world began to see purely regional conflicts that Central American governments attempted to resolve in a peaceful, humane, orderly fashion. The peace plan ultimately forced the Sandinista regime to hold democratic elections and relinquish power. Since the change in the government to the north, Costa Rica has resumed normal relations with Nicaragua. Although not obeyed to the letter by those who signed it, the peace plan has become a prototype for regional problem-solving.

146

List of Photographs

151

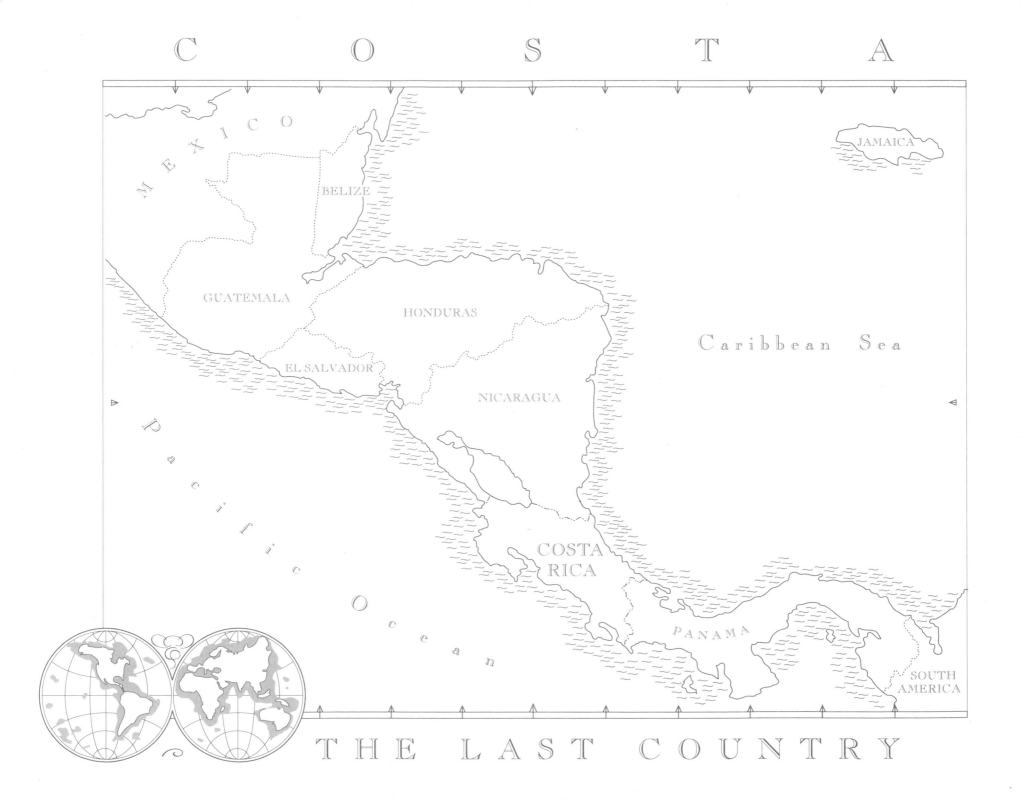

C O S T A

MEXICO

BELIZE

JAMAICA

GUATEMALA

HONDURAS

Caribbean Sea

EL SALVADOR

NICARAGUA

COSTA
RICA

PANAMA

SOUTH
AMERICA

Pacific Ocean

THE LAST COUNTRY